Reviewed by the
Parent-Teacher Advisory Board

Developmental Overview by Nancy Richard

becker & mayer!
BOOKS

A FIRESIDE BOOK
Published by Simon & Schuster

JENNIFER RICHARD JACOBSON
AND DOTTIE RAYMER

How Is My *Fifth Grader* Doing in School?

WHAT TO EXPECT AND HOW TO HELP

Fireside
Rockefeller Center
1230 Avenue of the Americas
New York, NY 10020

becker & mayer!
BOOKS

Produced by becker&mayer!
www.beckermayer.com

Copyright © 2000 by Jennifer Richard Jacobson and Dottie Raymer
All rights reserved, including the right of reproduction in whole or in part in any form.

FIRESIDE and colophon are registered trademarks of Simon & Schuster Inc.

becker&mayer! and colophon are trademarks of becker&mayer!, Ltd.

Manufactured in the United States of America

1 3 5 7 9 10 8 6 4 2

Library of Congress Cataloging-in-Publication Data
Jacobson, Jennifer, date.
How is my fifth grader doing in school? : what to expect and how to help /
by Jennifer Richard Jacobson and Dottie Raymer.
p. cm.
Includes index.
1. Fifth grade (Education)—United States. 2. Education, Elementary—Parent
participation—United States. 3. Parent-teacher relationshps—United States.
4. Mathematics—Study and teaching (Elementary)—United States. 5. Language arts
(Elementary)—United States. I. Title. II. Raymer, Dottie.

LB1571 5th .J23 2000
372.24'2 21—dc21   99-044992
ISBN 0-684-84714-0

Acknowledgments

We would like to give special thanks to Nancy Richard, who wrote the Developmental Overview for this book. Nancy has been a student of child development, school readiness, and effective classroom practices for the past thirty years. She has worked with thousands of teachers and parents throughout the country to promote classrooms that are educationally successful as well as responsive to the developmental needs of children. She has served on the national lecture staff of the Gesell Institute of Human Development and has been a consulting teacher for the Northeast Foundation for Children. She co-authored the book *One Piece of the Puzzle: A School Readiness Manual.*

We would also like to thank Rosie Bensen for her "imagineering." As a teacher, writer, and mother of two, Rosie created and successfully implemented many activities presented in this book. She has inspired countless students of art and writing, and we are grateful for her boundless vision.

In addition, we would like to thank the members of our Parent-Teacher Advisory Board who volunteered hours and hours to reading and critiquing the books in this series. They have graciously shared their educational knowledge and insight. Their wisdom, gathered through years of working with children in classrooms, has enriched these books tremendously. Their guidance has been invaluable. Members of the Parent-Teacher Advisory Board are as follows:

Jim Grant, a former teacher and principal, is an internationally known consultant and one of America's most passionate advocates for children. He is the founder of the Society for Developmental Education, the nation's primary provider of staff development training for elementary teachers. He is also founder and co-executive director of the National Alliance of Multiage Educators and the author of dozens of professional articles and educational materials. His books *"I Hate School!" Some Common-Sense Answers for Educators and Parents Who Want to Know Why and What to Do About It, Retention and Its Prevention,* and *A Common-Sense Guide to Multiage Practices* are recognized resources for teachers, parents, and administrators.

Mary Mercer Krogness, a public school teacher for over thirty years, is the recipient of the Martha Holden Jennings Master Teacher Award, the highest recognition the foundation bestows on a classroom teacher in Cleveland, Ohio. She has taught grades k–8 in both urban and suburban schools and is currently a language arts consultant for five school systems, an educational speaker, and an author. In addition to award-winning articles, Mary is the author of *Just Teach Me, Mrs. K: Talking, Reading, and Writing with Resistant Adolescent Learners* and is the writer-producer of an award-winning, nationally disseminated PBS television series, *Tyger, Tyger, Burning Bright,* a creative writing program for elementary age students.

Connie Plantz, an elementary school teacher for over twenty years, has had extensive experience with students of economic, academic, and cultural diversity. In addition to being a classroom teacher, she has held the titles of grade level leader, reading specialist, teacher of gifted and talented students, and chairperson of the Multicultural Committee. She has developed curricula and acted as an educational consultant for homeschoolers and educational publishing companies, and has taught graduate courses in reading and teacher education at National University. Connie also reviews children's literature and is the author of fiction and nonfiction, including *Pacific Rim,* for middle grade readers.

Robert (Chip) Wood, is the co-founder of the Northeast Foundation for Children, a nonprofit educational foundation whose mission is the improvement of education in elementary and middle schools. The foundation provides training, consultation, and professional development opportunities for teachers and administrators. It also operates a k–8 laboratory school for children and publishes articles and books (by teachers) for educators and parents. Chip has served NEFC as a classroom teacher, consultant, and executive director. He is the author of many professional articles and the book *Yardsticks: Children in the Classroom, Ages 4–14,* and co-author of *A Notebook for Teachers: Making Changes in the Elementary Curriculum.*

It takes many people to create a book. We would like to thank the talented staff at becker & mayer who produced this book, especially Jim Becker, who offered this idea; Andy Mayer, who has followed it through; Jennifer Worick, who graciously navigated this book through all channels; Simon Sung, who coordinated art; Heidi Baughman, who designed the assessment booklet; Jennifer Doyle, who worked with panel members; Dan Minnick, who drew computer sketches; and Kelly Skudlarick, who worked on the original proposal.

We would also like to acknowledge the members of the Simon & Schuster publishing group, particularly Trish Todd, who has shared our vision and commitment to this series; Cherise Grant, who has been engaged in all aspects of production; Barbara Marks, who designed the book; Toni Rachiele, production editor; and Marcela Landres, who did a little bit of everything.

And finally we would like to thank the many teachers, parents, and children who have offered their knowledge, anecdotes, insights, artwork, and advice. We hope you recognize your contributions on these pages.

for Kelly, Sara, Sam, and Peter—J.R.J.

for Willie and Elsie—D.E.R.

Contents

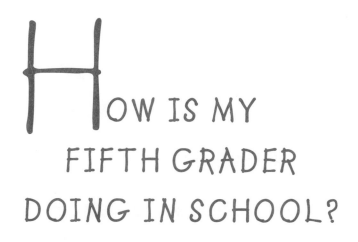

How is my fifth grader doing in school?

Introduction

Even if your child does not yet attend an official middle school, it is likely that both you and your child's teacher think of fifth grade as the year to increase your child's independence and responsibility. In many ways the timing seems right. Your fifth grader appears more pulled together and organized this year. He might even be telling you that it's time for him to take more control of his life.

On the other hand, your child has burst into tears three evenings this week. Apparently, she has two places in school to keep her belongings and she can never remember which locker her assignments are in. At night you are advising her to call her friend for information regarding homework or trying to piece together her understanding of her teacher's expectations. During the day you are receiving calls from your child about an instrument that's been left in the front hall, a required permission slip you knew nothing about, or a lunch that was left on the bus. Before long, you are frustrated with your child, your child's teacher, or both. Perhaps you sense that your child's teacher is equally frustrated with you.

What does this mean? It usually means that, yes, your child is ready to take more responsibility for her schoolwork but she still needs a good deal of guidance, modeling, and support. In other words, she still needs your steady and attentive involvement in her school life.

Far too many parents believe that once their child enters middle school their years of involvement in their child's education are over. This belief works against children, often with detrimental results. Parent participation is a leading component of school success. Children from all socioeconomic backgrounds are happier, more motivated, and get better grades when their parents take an active role in helping them to learn.

So how do you help the fifth grader to learn? By helping him to develop regular study habits and routines, by listening attentively to how he thinks about what he is learning so you can help him develop new strategies and clear up misconceptions, by using those five- or ten-minute teachable moments at home to introduce or reinforce a concept, and by showing up regularly at your child's school. This book can help you be effective in all of these ways—even if your time with your child is extremely short. This book won't give you more time, but it will help you use the time you have more creatively. Ultimately you will find that the time you do spend learning with your child is enriched and remarkably rewarding for both of you.

How Is My Fifth Grader Doing in School? comes with an observational assessment that will help you determine what in the traditional fifth grade curriculum your child knows and what might be helpful to introduce to her next. This assessment is not a standardized test. It is not an IQ test. In this assessment, you will not find any quantifiable scores or percentiles. Instead, you will find ways for you to observe how your child approaches learning. If you watch carefully, you might find the results surprising.

As with all the books in this series, the learning activities in *How Is My Fifth Grader Doing in School?* cover the broad strokes of the fifth grade reading, writing, and math curriculum. Science, social studies, the arts, or physical education are not covered because the content in these subjects varies from school to school and cannot be presented accurately. Nevertheless, they are essential to a sound education, and your child needs to know that you value these subjects as well. Find out what your child is studying in these areas and see if there is a way you can contribute. Explore new knowledge in science and social studies, go to museums, attend concerts and plays. Discover how rewarding learning with your child can be.

Developmental Overview

by Nancy Richard

Fifth grade is viewed as a paradoxical year: one moment the children seem to be entrenched in the innocence of childhood; the next, portraying the traits associated with beginning adolescence. In this year of passage, most fifth graders are happily grounded in the security of familiar childhood routines and patterns, while at the same time beginning to reach out to find their own identities.

Not all children in the fifth grade are alike, nor will they learn in the same way. Every child is unique. In any grade, children will range in age. It is also important to remember that your child has an individual rate of growth as well as an individual pattern of growth that must be respected. Some children grow fast—others, more slowly. However, because of school law, most fifth graders will be ten to eleven years old at the beginning of the school year, eleven to eleven and a half at the end. The curriculum of fifth grade is geared to this age and this stage of development.

As children differ, so do schools. Some fifth grades are self-contained with one or two teachers. Others are in multiage configurations. Still others are housed in middle schools where the children have multiple teachers. Also, classes differ from year to year, school to school. Good teachers at this age level understand and work with the complexities of the age, but they also use the strengths of the age to help children learn.

Love of Movement

In her awesome and ingenious design for human development, Mother Nature seems to emphasize one aspect of growth at one stage, another aspect at another stage. In the fifth grade, a noticeable characteristic is the need for lots of activity and movement. Fifth graders love to be outdoors running and chasing each other.

Most fifth graders like nothing better than to play. When they come home from school, they have barely time to change their clothes and grab a snack before they're bolting out of doors to hop on their bikes, go rollerblading, or join their friends in shooting baskets. These are just a few of the activities that engage them. Very fond of their neighborhood buddies, they love neighborhood games—such as red rover, capture the flag, and tag—that involve racing and chasing.

One would expect, then, with all this love of movement, that physical education would be a favorite subject in school. Most fifth graders look forward to it, but it often creates a dilemma for them. Should they compete or not compete? On one hand, they want to be a part of the group and they try to not exclude anyone or hurt anyone's feelings. On the other hand, they want to be seen by their peers as competent in sports, and even when cooperation is stressed, they will compete vigorously.

This is an age when sports heroes emerge. In team sports, then, they will blame the less competent players if the team doesn't win. They will brag when they do well: "I was the best." To deal with this dilemma, some schools allow only cooperative games to be played in fifth grade and set up situations where fifth graders can show off their skills by competing against themselves.

This need for movement can create other problems in school if the teacher isn't sensitive to it. Unable to sit in their seats for long periods of time, fifth graders need to shift activities often. They need frequent breaks for movement—in the afternoon, especially—and they can get very "antsy" if there is no recess or built-in activity in the curriculum. Some teachers will plan science and social studies around hands-on activities and field trips. Others will plan periods of time for structured movement such as yoga, tai chi, or calisthenics.

Naturalists

Besides being outside for fun, fifth graders want to be out of doors for another reason. Many are very fond of nature and want to be a part of it. They like exploring their immediate environment, as well as learning about environments that are different from their own. They are interested in conservation and environmental problems and will participate in efforts to improve the environment. They even like studying environmental problems on a global scale. Some children at this age create nature trails; others like cleaning up a park or planting and watching things grow. Some children at this age like observing and classifying birds or fish. Almost all are interested in animals.

Most fifth graders like adventure. They also like learning survival skills and will seek out books with these themes. Fifth grade is a time when children will find a special spot for themselves in the park or woods, in a hedge, or in a tree. These cherished places become their houses, dens, and forts. This is a highlight year for Boy Scouts and Girl Scouts, and just about the best year for summer camp.

Perhaps connected to this love of the environment is another predominant trait: a desire to help people and animals. Many fifth graders aspire to one of the helping professions such as teaching or medicine. Becoming a veterinarian is especially popular. While they love animals of all kinds, boys seem content with dogs, while horses are by far the favorite of the girls. Much to the chagrin of their parents, some fifth graders will spend the year begging for a dog or a horse.

Looking for a good survival story? Try one of these:

- *Earthquake,* by Peg Kehret (Cobblehill)
- *Hatchet,* by Gary Paulsen (Simon & Schuster)
- *Island of the Blue Dolphins,* by Scott O'Dell (Dell)
- *Lost on a Mountain in Maine,* by Donn Fendler (Beech Tree)
- *The Talking Earth* and *Julie of the Wolves,* by Jean Craighead George (HarperCollins)
- *Walks Alone,* by Brian Burks (Harcourt Brace)

Relating to Parents

Family is very important to fifth graders. They love to talk about their families, and their writing often contains family stories. They will make up original stories about family life. They especially love family get-togethers and outings: holidays, picnics, and reunions. These outings often provide cherished lifelong memories.

Although they are not very good at helping around the house, and not always nice to siblings, usually fifth graders are pleasant to have around. They are affectionate and companionable, and will sometimes spontaneously give a parent a hug or a kiss. Close to parents in general, they try to be good and are usually both obedient and loyal to family values.

There *are* a couple of traits often seen in fifth graders that *do* bother parents. One is bathing. Fifth graders often have difficulty leaving their play to take a bath. In some households this can become a battle. It's best to schedule a bath for certain times on certain nights—and then stick to it. For most parents and children, the issue of bathing will disappear in a year or two. It's difficult to get adolescents *out* of the shower.

Another issue is clothing. Not only do they leave it on the floor or piled on a chair, they usually don't like new clothing and prefer old and comfortable outfits. Clothing might still be an issue next year, but it will be of a different nature. Instead of wearing clothes for comfort, most sixth graders will emulate the "in" clothing of the peer group.

Ten-to-eleven-year-olds are also not very good at cleaning their rooms. However, most are good at taking direction and will accept your help and supervision in room cleanup on a Saturday morning. However, the job of cleaning the whole room is too much for most of them; they need specific tasks to do, such as putting away their collections or hanging up their clothes.

Fifth graders are beginning to see that other children's homes and families are different from their own, with different outlooks and standards. They like to go to their friends' houses to observe differences in both the physical environment and style of living. They make comparisons in nonjudgmental ways: "I went to Michael's. His house is big."

This curiosity about home and lifestyles extends beyond their immediate boundaries to children in other areas of the country, to other countries, to different cultures. Fifth graders like to connect with other children through writing letters or on the Internet to find out about family life and traditions.

Relating to Friends

Fifth graders are friendly and expect others to be friendly also. They love their friends, especially neighborhood buddies, and usually get along with them. At school, they enjoy playing together, and they will lovingly poke fun at each other and even share in the embarrassment of a friend. They are trying out relationships, and the configuration of their friendships changes often.

Ten-to-eleven-year-olds are beginning to invest in the peer group, noting the current fashion in clothing and footwear. However, they are still more loyal to parents than to friends and will abide by their parents' wishes. They strive to develop a style and identity of their own on the one hand, but are unwilling to break away from parents' viewpoints on the other. They still need the emotional protection of their parents' perspective. They will listen to friends, consider their views, and then take the safe position of "my mother said" or "my father said."

Fifth grade is a time when the sexes begin to show differences in handling problems in relationships. The boys, who relate more through camaraderie and doing things together, will occasionally have outbursts of anger in which they call names, stamp their feet, or even strike out. These outbursts are usually quickly forgotten, however.

Many of the girls are approaching puberty, especially toward the end of the year, and interpersonal relationships are becoming increasingly important to them. Because of this, any slight (or imagined slight) by a friend, any misunderstanding or unkind gossip, can cause them to be angry or hurt. They often show this anger or hurt by not speaking or not playing. Some girls can get over these tiffs quickly and not hold a grudge, but many will carry the anger or hurt all day long. Unfortunately, the cliques that are so prevalent in middle school are beginning.

These interpersonal issues of friendships, cliques, anger, and hurt feelings, as well as responsibility for each other, need to be addressed. If they aren't, school can begin to be a nightmare for many children. It is helpful if your child's school helps children work out these issues as part of the curriculum. Many schools are teaching children how to solve interpersonal problems in peaceful ways. You might check with your child's school to see if conflict resolution is a high priority.

If these issues aren't addressed in your child's class, however, it is important that you talk about these issues with her. How is she handling her hurt and anger? How can she keep from hurting her classmates? Fifth graders, especially, like to role-play. Set up some scenarios with your child and brainstorm some solutions.

Beginning sexual awareness is also expressed differently by the sexes. Many boys burp, break wind, make a similar noise with their armpits, and giggle about anything having to do with sex or other bodily functions. They often tell smutty jokes—even though they sometimes don't really understand them.

Most girls express their budding sexuality by being very private about their bodies, even in their families. They are reticent to talk about sex and are often embarrassed about receiving sex information, even though they need it.

Fifth graders want to be good, to be fair, to be nice to everyone. But very often they do not have the social skills to carry this off. This year is an excellent one in which to teach them how to communicate with each other and how to express their feelings. They love talking about things that are important to them, and they are eager for direction at this stage. In another year, giving social direction will be much more difficult.

Relating to Teachers

Fifth grade children will usually express affection for and accept affection from their teachers. In fact, many fifth graders fall in love with a teacher and think he or she can do no wrong. On the other hand, a fifth grader might hate his teacher. There seems to be very little middle ground here. Those children having more than one teacher often discuss the characteristics of their teachers, and what makes a good teacher.

Because fifth graders are highly sensitive to how the teacher treats them and others (and easily hurt by criticism), it is very important to them that their teacher be firm, fair, and friendly. They feel safe when he is definitely in charge. They like a teacher to set the standards, and they try hard to live up to those standards. They also like a teacher who keeps to a schedule. Knowing what's coming next gives them a feeling of security.

At school, fifth graders are willing to take the consequences of any rule infractions, but the consequences must be immediate, fair, and last for only a short time. They also want the consequences *right now!* They cannot stand long-term or delayed punishments. You will probably see this need for immediacy at home as well. Many ten-to-eleven-year-olds want to do everything in the now: "I'm hungry and I want to eat *right now!*" "I need to call Jessie *right now!*"

Somewhat reminiscent of their preschool years, some fifth graders can't handle seeing two people in authority (parent and teacher) together at the same time. You might find that your child has difficulty, perhaps acts more babyish, when you visit school unexpectedly or informally. However, in a planned and controlled situation—such as a production they are putting on or an author's tea they are involved in—most fifth graders love having you at school.

Schoolwork

Most fifth graders are curious but also literal and factual. They like dealing with specifics and don't easily generalize. They are apt to skim the surface of things and tend not to be analyzers. Moreover, many are not yet abstract thinkers but are reality bound, and because of this, the more the curriculum can reflect the real world, the better. Math problems dealing with shopping, money, and comparison buying make sense to them. They like to apply skills to the solution of problems in a concrete and practical way.

The fifth grade math curriculum usually deals heavily with decimals and fractions. These can be very difficult for children who are not yet able to think abstractly. In order for them to get a real understanding of fractions, most fifth graders need concrete objects to work out problems. Because they are action oriented, they often learn best when the lessons can be connected to bodily movement and games, such as using jump rope rhymes to learn the multiplication tables.

In the beginning of the year, word problems that have several operations—for instance, addition and division—in the same problem give fifth graders trouble. It is almost as if they have compartments in their minds and can't cross over. They take comfort in worksheets that involve only one operation at a time. At the end of the year, however, new abilities of abstraction and generalization are emerging, and they enjoy oral arithmetic—where they can use their knowledge of number facts and make quick mental shifts.

Although most fifth graders have difficulty with abstract thought, they do have some other gifts that can be used to help them learn. Memory is one. Fifth graders will memorize long poems and recite them with expression. They will memorize facts and dates; state capitals, flowers, and birds; math facts; play parts; football or baseball statistics. Spelling might be a favorite subject. They like to show off the facts they know and will often start their sentences with "Did you know . . . ?" Atlases and the *Guinness Book of World Records* are favorite resources.

Another intellectual gift often seen in fifth grade, and the forerunner of abstract thinking, is the ability to see relationships and to express them in concrete ways. Some represent these relationships through writing, others through drawing and map work, and others through building and constructing.

Fifth graders are good listeners and especially like listening to stories. They like starting the school day with a story. Although their writing is often sloppy, they like to take dictation (a practice used to assess children's understanding of writing mechanics but not seen in many classrooms today). They are also talkers and like to tell stories about something they've seen or heard. They draw from their personal experience and like to talk about themselves and their families. Discussion on a subject can go on and on if not limited by an adult with a few well-timed questions.

Homework

Homework? Fifth graders don't like it! They want to play when they aren't in school. For most of them, this will be the last year of childhood tumbling, wrestling, and chasing. Although they don't know this, Mother Nature does, and calls them to it.

Most schools, however, demand homework, and it can be a problem for child and parent alike. Although fifth graders have few immediate worries, they do worry about the responsibility of homework. It will help your child if you plan together a very specific daily homework time. Usually right after school will not work, and neither will early evening if you live in a neighborhood where children are safe out of doors in the evening. Homework will be done hurriedly and sloppily in the rush to play.

Rather, plan a time between bath and bedtime that's held exclusively for homework. Homework should not take more than 50 minutes per day. If your child is sticking to the task, and if it's taking longer than 50 minutes to finish it, a conference with the teacher is in order. Perhaps some adjustment is necessary. Fifth graders want to please parents and teachers—and *want* their homework to be done well. They try to be responsible but still need help with timing.

In their eagerness to play, sometimes children will say they have *no* homework, when in actuality they have a long-range project that doesn't have to be in tomorrow but *does* have to be in at the end of the week. It is helpful for them to still put in their usual half hour each night, rather than hurriedly doing the whole project at the last minute. Also, they will worry less about getting it done.

Enjoying Your Fifth Grader

This is a year to take as much time as you can to really know and enjoy your child. For most children, fifth grade is their last year to bask in the innocence and adventure of childhood. Likewise, for most parents, it is the last year to be with your child without some struggle for quite a while. For most parents and children, not until about junior year in high school will life be as good again.

Right now, your child admires you, likes being with you, and is frank, open, and friendly. He asks you for permission to do things, is obedient and predictable. He's also interesting and full of information. What more could a parent ask? In these times of busy schedules, it's often hard to find the time just to be with your child, but it's very important to him that you do. Above all, savor this year and have fun!

Questions and Answers About Fifth Grade

My daughter is a voracious reader—reads everything she can get her hands on. But we have to coax and cajole our fifth grade son to get him to read anything. It's not that he's not a good reader, it's just that he won't read. Any suggestions?

Yours is not an uncommon problem. Sometime around the fourth or fifth grade, as many as *one third* of all children in school stop reading. For some reason, these perfectly competent readers simply lose interest. There are many reasons why this happens. For one, a child's life becomes increasingly active during these years. For another, fifth graders crave social interaction. Friends, clubs, sports, and extracurricular events take precedence over time to read. Boys in particular receive the cultural message that while engaging in sports is a perfectly acceptable way to spend your free time, reading is not. And while girls will socialize around books—they discuss them, give their opinions, and share books they read (some belong to the new upcrop of book clubs for girls)—boys seldom do.

A third reason many children slow down in their reading during the middle school years is that parents stop reading to and with their children. To make matters worse, most children never see their parents read. This communicates the mistaken message that reading is not one of the desirable leisure activities, that reading is something you might do if you were stranded on a desert island perhaps, or if it rained for seven straight days. So how do you counter these influences? Here are a couple of suggestions:

➤ Continue reading aloud to your child. Fifth graders, despite the independent stance they try to take once in a while, still crave one-to-one time with their parents. Reading good books together will give you and your child the opportunity to "talk books," one of the most effective ways to develop the thinking skills necessary to progress in reading. When your child hits adolescence, you will look back on these times you read and shared together without a moment's regret.

➤ Schedule a family **DEAR** time, when everyone in the family will "Drop Everything And Read." Be vigilant about keeping this time. Any time you knock it out of the schedule you communicate that something else was more important.

Read the Reading Comprehension section beginning on page 60 for more specific ways to ignite the reading flame in your child.

I was never very good at math myself, and, frankly, I don't understand a lot of the math my child is bringing home. What can I do?

You don't need to know specific math procedures to help your child like mathematics and become a good problem solver. Remember, nobody's grading *you*! Even if your own math education was a nightmare, there are many ways you can help your child in math. Look through the list below and see if any make sense for your situation. Also check the chapter "Working with Your Child's Teacher" and some of the general suggestions listed in the chapter "Working Below Grade Level in Math." Above all, remember to try to keep a positive attitude. Making math a battleground or a field of anxiety won't be good for either your child's math skills or your parent-child relationship.

➤ Don't pass along your anxiety. You might be tempted to commiserate ("I always hated math, too!"), but block that urge. Contrary to popular opinion, there is no such thing as a math gene. Don't give your child the opportunity to think she inherited an inability to do math from you.

➤ Assume that your child's math work is going to take some time. Any problem worth its salt takes a while to figure out. Act as if there is nothing you would rather do than sit down and grapple with the problem at hand. Who knows, with the right attitude and a chocolate chip cookie, it might turn out to be fun!

➤ Admit that you don't know the answer. Say, "Wow! We sure didn't study this when *I* was in fifth grade!" Let your child be the teacher for a change and explain it to you. There is no better way of making sure you understand a concept than to try to teach it to someone else.

➤ Don't assume that you have to teach your child. If your child doesn't understand a homework assignment, help her read through it carefully and try to isolate the confusing parts. Suggest that she look at the problem from a different angle, perhaps by drawing a picture or acting out the problem. But do not assume that you have to do the math for her. If she (and you) is still stumped, write a quick note to her teacher explaining that your child has put a lot of good thought and time into trying to come up with a solution. Encourage your child to ask the teacher for extra help—and then don't forget to ask your child for the solution!

➤ Keep learning. Look upon the upcoming years as an opportunity to pick up a few of the skills you missed along the way. Let your child see you doing math in your everyday life. If you are struggling with a problem, let her see that, too, and consider asking her for help in solving your dilemma. Your child needs to know that solving problems takes persistence, spunk, and energy. And remember, no matter what your preadolescent might say, you are still her first and foremost model.

➤ If you are truly frozen by math anxiety, the following books might ease your mind—or at least convince you that you are not alone. Pick one up at your local library.
  • *Fear of Math,* by Claudia Zaslavsky (Rutgers University Press)
  • *Math Anxiety,* by Sheila Tobias (Norton)
  • *Math: Facing an American Phobia,* by Marilyn Burns (Math Solutions Publications)

➤ Above all, continue to involve your child in the cheerful, informal process of doing math around your house. Cook with her, build with her, talk about the latest baseball statistics or the weather report. Use the informal, five-minute activities in this book to slip math into your daily routine. After a while, you might even forget you're doing math!

I noticed that a calculator was on my child's list of school supplies this year. If kids are using calculators in school, how are they ever going to learn to do calculations on their own?

Before we get into the subject of calculators, think about the math you do in your daily life. How many times do you solve a problem with a quick mental calculation? When do you use pen and paper? When do you pull out a calculator? How often do you just make your best guess or a good estimate?

By fifth grade, most students are beginning to make judgments about when it makes sense to use a calculator and when it's easier to turn to another calculation method. They have enough number sense to know that 400 minus 1 is 399 without having to write it down or use the calculator. They know that a calculator can't tell you what to do with a remainder in a division problem and that it is almost useless when it comes to calculating with fractions. Fifth graders, always up for a bit of competition, also know that if they know their math facts they can get to the answer for 7 times 8 faster than anyone will ever get to it on a calculator.

Still, a calculator is a valuable teaching tool, just as pencil and paper are tools. Calculators allow children to focus on interesting problem solving even when the numbers get unwieldy. They allow children to explore patterns, to play with negative numbers, and to keep numbers in memory that normal brain cells would immediately reject. If you are concerned about calculators in your child's classroom, visit a math class and see for yourself how they are being used. Remember that the problems your child will be solving in the future are more complex than you might imagine today. Your child will need to have experience with a full range of tools—including calculators—to solve these problems, and the sooner she learns when and how to use those tools appropriately, the better.

My child's teacher often offers "extra credit" assignments, but my fifth grader refuses to do them. Sometimes she lies by telling me the teacher didn't give a bonus question. I want her to do the best she can in school, but I don't want to push.

Imagine how frustrating it is for a fifth grader to know that not only does she have to complete homework every night (something most fifth graders resent) but now her teacher has gone and raised the bar. In order to succeed, she has to do extra work. Some children will be motivated by such a plan, others will simply let it go. They discover that the world won't come to an end if they don't complete that extra bonus question—and, in fact, they'll get fifteen extra minutes of play instead.

You might do well to take the pressure off your child. Children need down time. Let your child know that you honor her time to be physically active, to dream quietly, to cook up delightful schemes. These open-ended activities will foster the self-direction, creativity, resilience, and flexibility of thought your child will need in the years ahead.

In the meantime, focus on the big picture. Ultimately, you do not want your child to simply strive for external rewards—the next good grade. You want her to become truly interested and excited about learning. You want her to tackle that bonus question, not because her teacher will know she's smart but because she simply has to know the answer, has fun doing projects, or because she loves being challenged.

Begin by helping her to feel her *present* success in learning. Instead of focusing on what she could be doing, focus on what she *is* doing. Point out all of the ways she has demonstrated her skill and thoughtfulness as a learner. Be as specific as you can, so she will trust your feedback and not feel manipulated by it. For instance, instead of saying "This is a wonderful book report. See how smart you are?" you might say, "You said that you liked this book because it's about friendship. Recognizing the theme of a book, the main thing it's about, is a difficult skill. Well done." Tell her how proud you are of her achievements big and small. Remember, a leading factor of school success is feeling successful.

How to Use This Book

Using the Parent Observation Pages and the For Kids Only Booklet

Assessment is a natural process for parents. Every time you asked your young child a question—"Can you say Dada?" "Where is your nose?" "What color is this?"—you were collecting information and using that information to determine what to teach your child next. If you had questions about your child's development, you asked your pediatrician or consulted a checklist of developmental stages of learning. By observing your child and asking the right questions, you were able to support your child's learning.

Now that your child is school-aged, however, you might find it harder to maintain the role of supportive coach. It's a greater challenge to get a clear understanding of what is expected of your child. Without specific knowledge of the curriculum, you might not know what questions to ask. The purpose of this book, and of the accompanying assessment, is to help you to observe your child with awareness again.

The word *assessment* comes from roots that mean "to sit beside." The informal assessment is a way for you to sit beside your child and collect the information you need. After you have observed your child, you will be guided to activities that will encourage you and your child to continue to learn together.

Remember, the assessment is not a standardized test. It will not tell you how your child compares to other children in the nation. It will not even tell

32

you how your child compares with your neighbor's child. But it will give you a starting point for determining how to increase your child's confidence and success in learning. Instructions for participating in the assessment are as follows:

1. **Take the For Kids Only Booklet out of the envelope in the back of the book and read through it one time.** This will familiarize you with the visuals that you will be presenting to your child.

2. **Photocopy and read the Parent Observation Pages (page 36).** Reading these pages ahead of time will help you to see how the child's booklet and your instructions are coordinated. It will also allow you to determine how long it might take your child to complete it. For the fifth grade assessment we recommend doing an activity here or there over at least a week's time. As you will see, the beginning of the reading assessment requires your immediate participation. You will probably be able to complete this section in one five-minute sitting. The rest of the reading, writing, and math assessments can be done independently by your child and will require, considering a fifth grader's busy schedule and the thoroughness of the assessment, several relaxed sessions. Remember, most fifth graders like to take their time and complete an activity carefully.

   Keep in mind also that this book covers the skills your child will be introduced to over a full year of learning. If you give your child the assessment at the beginning of the school year, the results will obviously be different than if you give the assessment at the end of the year. Teachers introduce the material at different times. So don't be anxious if your child tells you that he's never heard of an idiom or an algebraic equation. Be pleased that you can introduce these terms in a fun and lively way at home.

3. **Give your child the For Kids Only Booklet. Provide a place to give the assessment that is relatively free of distractions.** Show your child how the assessment works. Tell your child that you want to learn more about him and that these activities will teach *you*. Let him know that after he completes the assessment, the book will direct you both to fun activities. Make sure you approach the activity in a lighthearted manner.

   Don't approach your child expecting him or her to balk. Most preadolescent children wish their parents would talk about and help them with their schoolwork more often. Let your child know that you want to help in any way you can.

4. **Above all, keep the assessment fun and relaxed for your child.** If your child is afraid to try an activity, don't push him. After all, that is valuable information for you, too. Whenever your child has difficulty with a

reading passage or a math problem, *stop* and skip ahead to the question directed (or the one that immediately follows). There is never a reason to work beyond your child's comfort level.

5. **Give positive reinforcement as often as possible.** You might just say, "I didn't know you could do that!" If your child seems upset or confused by an exercise, let him off the hook. You might say, "That question is real confusing, isn't it?" Make sure your child ends the assessment feeling successful. One way of doing this is to return to a question your child could answer with obvious ease. Say, "I forgot to write your answer down. Can you show me how you did this problem again?"

Using the Assessment Guide

The assessment guide (page 53) will allow you to find out what your child knows and what he is ready to learn next. If you find that a question on the assessment did not give you enough information, or if you are confused about your child's response, you might want to talk to your child's teacher. See page 183 for more information.

Using the Suggested Activities

In each skill area, activities are suggested under two headings: "Have Five Minutes?" and "Have More Time?" Some of the activities in the five-minute section are quick games that you and your child can play while waiting for dinner, riding in the car, or walking to the bus stop. Others are activities that you can explain in less than five minutes and then let your child complete on his own. Activities in the "Have More Time?" category require more planning or a longer time commitment on your part.

Do not feel that you should do every activity listed under a skill heading. A number of different activities are provided so you can pick and choose the ones that appeal to you and your child. And don't feel guilty if you haven't tried something new for a while. If you do only a couple of these activities occasionally, you will be giving your fifth grader a genuine boost toward success. You'll be amazed at how a question here or a three-minute activity there can demonstrate to your child how much you value his ideas and his education. Feel free to adapt these activities to your needs.

Even if you are not directed to a specific section, you might want to try some of the activities in that section. Reviewing has wonderful benefits. When your child revisits a skill, he usually gains a deeper understanding that he can apply to new learning. In every area there are sure to be games that your child will enjoy playing.

Should you pursue activities that seem more difficult? Probably not. Pushing your child too fast can backfire. Instead of looking forward to the games you initiate, your child might associate them with confusion, boredom, or failure. It's good to remember that success is the greatest motivator of all.

Some of the activities are competitive. Some fifth grade children do not care for competitive games. If your child is one, make the activity noncompetitive. Rather than playing against each other, make yourselves a team and try to beat the clock or another imaginary player—who always makes the most ridiculous decisions!

Repeat the assessment when appropriate

After some time has gone by—perhaps two or three months—and you and your child have participated in many of the activities, you might want to give the assessment, or a portion of it, again. By reassessing, you can determine if your child has grown in his understanding of concepts. It's possible that the Assessment Guide (page 53) will direct you to new areas of learning to focus on next.

If you choose not to give the entire assessment a second time, make sure you ask some questions that you know your child will answer competently. *Always end the assessment on a positive note.*

Remember, the assessment is meant to be an informal tool for gathering information. You might want to adapt the questions or ask new questions to see if your fifth grader has truly mastered a skill.

Many teachers now assess children in the classroom by doing what one educator termed kid watching. Kid watching is what parents have always done best. Have a ball watching your child grasp new knowledge.

Parent Observation Pages

....

Photocopy the Parent Observation Pages. Taking the time to photocopy the pages will allow you to match your child's responses to the answer guide more easily. It will also allow you to repeat the assessment on your child or to give the assessment to a sibling.

For additional information on using these pages and the rest of the assessment effectively, see "How to Use this Book," starting on page 32.

Reading Assessment and Writing Assessment

Ask your fifth grader to read the following passage titled "Dragon Slayer" **out loud**. (Choose a time when your child is rested and interested.) Count the number of words your child stops at or does not pronounce correctly. (Circle the words if you made a photocopy.) If your child goes back and corrects the pronunciation, or figures out the word on his or her own, do not count that word. If your child cannot determine the meaning of the word, provide the word and encourage him or her to continue reading.

DRAGON SLAYER

I looked down over the edge of the cliff, and there he was. His wingspan was wider than the fields behind my house. His eyes flashed molten yellow. He was the fiercest, most intimidating dragon I'd ever seen.

"Don't go down there, Caleb," my father yelled. "You don't stand a chance."

Perhaps I didn't stand half a chance of conquering that monster. But I had to try. Our home, our village, was in jeopardy. I tied a rope around my waist, checked the sword at my hip, and began to lower myself down.

That's when I woke up.

Do you ever have exciting dreams like this one? Scientists tell us that most people dream between three and five times a night. Each dream lasts from about ten to thirty minutes, and those that occur closer to waking tend to be longer than those that occurred earlier in the night. Some dreams are pleasant, others are bothersome, and some can be downright scary.

Most dreams involve events that happened during the day or strong wishes of the dreamer. Sometimes a sound, such as the alarm clock going off or the sound of dripping water, will make its way into a dream. What do you suppose caused this dreamer to dream of slaying dragons?

1. **Use the reading passage on page 37.** In your opinion, how well did your child read this passage? Please check one.
   ___ fluently ___ moderately well ___ slowly and haltingly

2. How many words did your child stop at (or was unable to determine or pronounce after a few moments)? Please check one.
   ___ 0–3 ___ 3–6 ___ more than 6

3. What does your child do to figure out a word he or she doesn't know? Check all that apply.
   ___ Sounds it out.
   ___ Divides the word into syllables.
   ___ Guesses based on context.
   ___ Skips the word and then goes back.
   ___ Knew all the words.

The For Kids Only Booklet, completed by your child, will provide the information you need to answer the remaining questions.

Show What You Know
Hint: You can look back at the story if you need to.
How would you classify this story?
___ realistic fiction ___ nonfiction ___ folktale

What was the problem in this story?_____
_____
_____

How did the main character solve the problem?___
_____
_____

Tell about one cause and effect relationship in this story.
Cause:_____
Effect:_____

What does the word *devour* mean?_____
What does the word *mirthful* mean?_____

Summarize this story:_____
_____
_____

4

Use assessment booklet page 4 for question 4.

4. **Use page 4 of the booklet.** Check all **correct** answers.
   ___ A. How would you classify this story? (folktale)
   ___ B. What was the problem in this story? (The Oni captured the old woman and didn't want her to leave.)
   ___ C. How did the main character solve the problem? (The woman ran away and/or she made faces at the Oni.)

_____ D. Tell about one cause-and-effect relationship in this story. (Some possible answers are: dumpling rolled down a hole/ woman followed it to another country; woman gave Oni a dumpling/Oni decided to make her his cook; woman made faces/Oni spit up river.)

_____ E. What does the word *devour* mean? (eat)

_____ F. What does the word *mirthful* mean? (cheerful)

_____ G. Summarize this story. (A woman chased her dumpling into another country. She was captured by an Oni, but she used her cleverness to escape.)

Use assessment booklet page 7 for question 5.

You Know the Drill!

What do you think the author's purpose was for writing this article?_____

What is the main idea of the article?_____
_____

Is the sentence, "They said that taking his medals had been an act of racism," a statement of fact or opinion?_____

Do you think Jim Thorpe should have been recognized as the winner of the gold medals?_____
_____

What is the suffix of *citizenship*?_____

Did you like reading this article? Why or why not?
_____
_____
_____

7

5. **Use page 7 of the booklet.** Check all **correct** answers.

_____ A. What do you think the author's purpose was for writing this article? (to inform the reader)

_____ B. What is the main idea of this article? (Jim Thorpe was a remarkable athlete.)

_____ C. Is the sentence, "They said that taking his medals had been an act of racism," a statement of fact or opinion? (fact)

_____ D. Do you think Jim Thorpe should have been recognized as the winner of the gold medals? (Check if your child gave a logical answer.)

_____ E. What is the suffix of *citizenship*? (ship)

_____ F. Did you like reading this article? Why or why not? (Check if your child explained his or her answer.)

Use page 9 of the booklet and any extra sheets your child might have added for question 6.

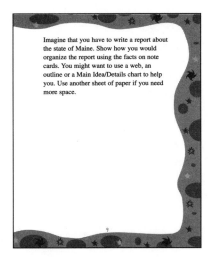

Imagine that you have to write a report about the state of Maine. Show how you would organize the report using the facts on note cards. You might want to use a web, an outline or a Main Idea/Details chart to help you. Use another sheet of paper if you need more space.

9

6. **Use page 9 of the booklet and any extra sheets your child might have added.** Check all that apply.
   ___ Child could organize the information using a personal method.
   ___ Procedure included organizing topics such as (but not restricted to) history, economics, and physical features.
   ___ Had difficulty categorizing the information.
   ___ Cannot organize this type of material at this time.

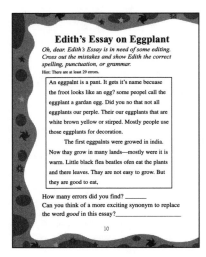

Edith's Essay on Eggplant
Oh, dear. Edith's Essay is in need of some editing. Cross out the mistakes and show Edith the correct spelling, punctuation, or grammar.
Hint: There are at least 29 errors.

An eggpalnt is a pant. It gets it's name becuase the froot looks like an egg? some peopel call the eggplant a gardan egg. Did you no that not all eggplants our perple. Their our eggplants that are white brown yellow or stirped. Mostly people use those eggplants for decoration.
     The first eggpalnts were growed in india. Now thay grow in many lands—mostly were it is warm. Little black flea beatles ofen eat the plants and there leaves. Thay are not easy to grow. But they are good to eat,

How many errors did you find? _____
Can you think of a more exciting synonym to replace the word *good* in this essay?_____

10

Use assessment booklet page 10 for question 7.

7. **Use page 10 of the booklet.** Circle the errors your child did *not* identify.

Edith's Essay on Eggplant

    eggplant   plant   its   because
An *eggpalnt* is a *pant*. It gets *it's* name *becuase*

fruit   . S   people
the *froot* looks like an egg*?* some *peopel* call the
        garden   know
eggplant a *gardan* egg. Did you *no* that not all
       are purple ? There are
eggplants *our perple. Their our* eggplants that are
     ,   ,   striped
white <u>brown</u> yellow or *stirped*. Mostly people use
those eggplants for decoration.
           eggplants   grown   India
The first *eggpalnts* were *growed* in *india.*
     they   where
Now *thay* grow in many lands—mostly *were* it is
                  beetles often
warm. Little black flea *beatles ofen* eat the plants
     their   They
and *there* leaves. *Thay* are not easy to grow. But
they   . or !
thay are good to eat,

Did your child come up with a synonym for *good?* ___ yes ___ no

*Use assessment
booklet page 11
for question 8.*

Reading Reactions

If you could guess, how many books would you
say you read last month? ____
How many did you have to read? ____
Why do you read?_____
_____
_____

Give each of the types of reading below a number.
Here are what the numbers mean:

1 - I love to read this.
2 - Sometimes I like to read this.
3 - I never read this.
4 - I have never tried this.
5 - I don't know what this is.

____ realistic fiction   ____ biographies
____ nonfiction   ____ magazine or news articles
____ science fiction   ____ poetry
____ fantasy   ____ comic books

My favorite author is _____ because_____
_____
_____.

11

8. **Use page 11 of the booklet.** Place your child's responses on the following reading rubric. It's possible that your child will not fall neatly into one category; perhaps she is a struggling reader emerging into a reader or a reader emerging into a lifelong reader (see the Assessment Guide, page 55, for additional explanations.) Given the following rubric, I would place my child as a _____.

	Struggling Reader	Reader	Lifelong Reader
Number of books read?	0–1	2–4	More than 3
How many books were read independently? (subtract number required from total)	0	1–3	More than 3
Why do you read?	"I have to"	Gives one personal reason (such as "It's fun")	Gives two or more personal reasons ("It's fun," "I learn things")
How many genres does your child love to read?	None	1–3	More than 3
Who is your favorite author?	Can't name one	Names favorite author	Names favorite author and gives a detailed explanation as to why

Have you ever been surprised? Really and truly? Write about a time when you were surprised. Use details to help the reader feel as if he or she was with you. Perhaps you can make your story or essay surprise the reader, too!_____

You can write more on the next page ➡

12

13

Use assessment booklet pages 12 to 14 for question 9.

9. **Use pages 12 to 14 of the booklet.** Use this writing sample to answer the following questions. Does your child's story show the following? (Check all that apply.)

_____ A. Approached this writing task with confidence.

_____ B. Considered the purpose of the story.

_____ C. Experimented with different ideas (plot, title, beginning, etc.).

_____ D. Expressed ideas clearly and in logical sequence.

_____ E. Used sensory details to help the reader imagine events.

_____ F. Used dialogue to show feelings and action.

_____ G. Wrote a captivating beginning and a satisfying conclusion.

_____ H. Took risks by using words that might or might not be spelled correctly.

_____ I. Made changes to the story to improve it. (You might need to ask your child if she or he made any changes.)

_____ J. Read it aloud to someone before considering it done.

_____ K. Wrote complete sentences.

_____ L. Avoided run-on sentences (long sentences that could be divided into a number of shorter sentences; run-on sentences usually contain too many "ands" or "buts").

_____ M. Used paragraph form.

_____ N. Used capitalization and punctuation properly.

_____ O. Used conventional spellings 90 percent of the time.

The Writing Reactions survey on page 15 of the booklet will also help you to assess your child's writing skills, comfort level, and needs. You will want to have it handy when using the Assessment Guide on page 53.

Math Assessment

Before beginning the math assessment, have paper and pencil available for your child to use. You might also wish to have a calculator to check your child's computation. Allow your child to work independently at his or her own pace—one or two pages at a time over the course of a few days is appropriate. Be available to help your child read the questions if necessary, but do not help your child solve the problems. If your child has difficulty with a problem, explain that not all fifth graders are expected to be able to solve all the problems and show him or her how to mark the "I haven't studied this yet" box at the bottom of the page.

Use assessment booklet pages 16 and 17 for question 1.

1. **Use pages 16 and 17 of the booklet.** Your child should have circled the following mistakes. *Check* all **incorrect** answers. *Circle* any problems your child did not attempt to solve.

a.
```
   82⑦
 - 199
   63②
```

c.
```
      8⑧ R 1
   7) 589
      56
      29
      28
       1
```

b.
```
     246
   x 587
    1722
   (1968)
   (1230)
    4920
```

d.
```
      4⑩ R 41
   42) 1763
      1680
        83
        42
        41
```

Correct answers:

a. 628   b. 144,402   c. 84 R 1   d. 41 R 41

Use assessment booklet page 18 for question 2.

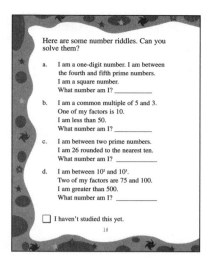

Here are some number riddles. Can you solve them?

a. I am a one-digit number. I am between the fourth and fifth prime numbers. I am a square number.
    What number am I? _____

b. I am a common multiple of 5 and 3. One of my factors is 10. I am less than 50.
    What number am I? _____

c. I am between two prime numbers. I am 26 rounded to the nearest ten.
    What number am I? _____

d. I am between 10^2 and 10^3. Two of my factors are 75 and 100. I am greater than 500.
    What number am I? _____

☐ I haven't studied this yet.

18

2. **Use page 18 of the booklet.** *Check* all **incorrect** answers. *Circle* any problems your child did not attempt to solve.

    a. 9   b. 30   c. 30   d. 600

Use assessment booklet page 19 for question 3.

Professor Bumble is stumped. He wants to use the numbers 2, 3, 4, and 5 to complete the following equations. Can you help him? Use any operations or groupings you want, but use **only** the numbers 2, 3, 4, and 5. You must use **all** the numbers in each equation and use each number only once.

Example: $(4 \times 5) + (2 + 3) = 25$

a. _____ = 120

b. _____ = 45

c. _____ = 2

d. _____ = 0

☐ I haven't studied this yet.

19

3. **Use page 19 of the booklet.** There are a number of possible solutions for each of these problems. Sample answers are given below. If necessary, use a calculator to check your child's equations. *Check* all **incorrect** answers. *Circle* any problems your child did not attempt to solve.

    a. $2 \times 3 \times 4 \times 5 = 120$
    b. $(2 + 3 + 4) \times 5 = 45$
    c. $(3 \times 4) - (2 \times 5) = 2$
    d. $(5 + 2) - (4 + 3) = 0$

Where do these numbers belong on the number line below? Write each one in its correct place on the number line.

| $1\frac{1}{4}$ | $\frac{1}{2}$ | 2.25 | .75 | $\frac{1}{8}$ |

0   1   2   3

Will the answers to the following problems be more or less than one? Circle the correct answer.

a. $\frac{1}{3} + \frac{1}{3} =$ more than one   less than one

b. $\frac{4}{5} + \frac{4}{5} =$ more than one   less than one

c. $\frac{3}{4} + \frac{3}{8} =$ more than one   less than one

d. $1\frac{1}{2} - \frac{3}{4} =$ more than one   less than one

e. $\frac{1}{2} \times \frac{1}{4} =$ more than one   less than one

f. $\frac{7}{8} \div \frac{1}{2} =$ more than one   less than one

☐ I haven't studied this yet.

20

Use assessment booklet page 20 for question 4.

4. **Use page 20 of the booklet.** *Check* all **incorrect** answers. *Circle* any problems your child did not attempt to solve.

0   ⅛   ½   .75   1   1¼   2   2.25   3

    a. less than one   d. less than one

    b. more than one   e. less than one

    c. more than one   f. more than one

Professor Bumble has a hole in his pocket, and now his change is all over the floor. He told his assistant that she could keep $\frac{1}{5}$ of any money she picked up. His assistant picked up 5 quarters, 6 dimes, 7 nickels, and 20 pennies. How much money did the assistant get to keep? _____

How did you figure out this problem? Show your work here.

☐ I haven't studied this yet.

21

Use assessment booklet page 21 for question 5.

5. **Use page 21 of the booklet.** *Check* the answer if it is **incorrect.** *Circle* the answer if your child did not attempt to solve the problem. Answer: 80¢.

Look at your child's work in the box. Check any of the following strategies your child appeared to use to solve the problem.

____ drew a picture

____ made a list

____ wrote an equation

____ guessed and checked

____ used actual coins

____ used logical reasoning (wrote calculations only)

If your child's answer was **incorrect**, look at his or her calculations. Check any that apply.

____ used incorrect operations (addition, subtraction, multiplication, division)

____ calculated money values incorrectly

____ calculated ⅓ of total incorrectly

Use assessment booklet page 22 for question 6.

> Can you solve these equations? Show your work on a separate sheet of paper.
>
> a. 8.758 + 6.82 = _____
>
> b. 88.7 - 14.623 = _____
>
> c. 13.7 x .54 = _____
>
> d. 34.785 ÷ 5 = _____
>
> Use decimal numbers to make up a word problem for someone else to solve. Check the other person's work. _____
>
> _____
> _____
> _____
> _____
> _____
>
> ☐ I haven't studied this yet.
>
> 22

6. **Use page 22 of the booklet.** *Check* all **incorrect** answers. *Circle* any problems your child did not attempt to solve.

   a. 15.578

   b. 74.077

   c. 7.398

   d. 6.957

After your child has written a problem, try to solve it. Then check all that apply:

____ Did not attempt to write a problem.

____ Began to write a problem, but did not know how to incorporate decimals.

(question continues)

____ Wrote a problem that did not incorporate decimals.

____ Wrote a story, but did not phrase it as a problem.

____ Wrote a problem that does not contain enough information.

____ Wrote an appropriate problem, but could not calculate the answer.

____ Wrote an appropriate problem and checked the answer correctly.

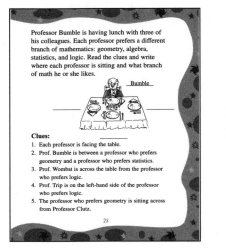

Use assessment booklet page 23 for question 7.

7. **Use page 23 of the booklet.** *Circle* any **incorrect** answers.

Bumble—logic

Clutz—
statistics

Trip—
geometry

Wombat—algebra

Ask your child how he or she went about solving the problem. Check all that apply.

____ Read and understood the problem.

____ Came up with a plan for solving the problem.

____ Seemed confident in his or her ability to solve the problem.

____ Used one or more of the following strategies:

    ____ used objects

    ____ drew a picture

    ____ made a chart

    ____ guessed and checked

    ____ used logical reasoning

    ____ Persisted until a solution was found

    ____ Attempted to solve the problem, but gave up quickly

    ____ Did not attempt to solve the problem

Use assessment booklet page 24 for question 8.

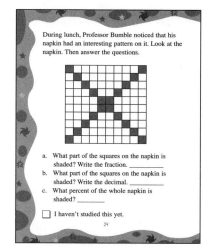

During lunch, Professor Bumble noticed that his napkin had an interesting pattern on it. Look at the napkin. Then answer the questions.

a. What part of the squares on the napkin is shaded? Write the fraction. _____
b. What part of the squares on the napkin is shaded? Write the decimal. _____
c. What percent of the whole napkin is shaded? _____

☐ I haven't studied this yet.

24

8. **Use page 24 of the booklet.** *Check* all **incorrect answers.** *Circle* any problems your child did not attempt to solve.
   a. ²⁰⁄₁₀₀ or ⅕
   b. .20 or .2
   c. 20%

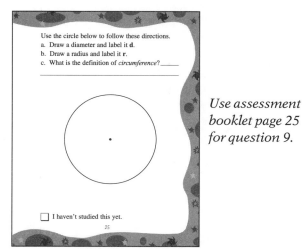

Use the circle below to follow these directions.
a. Draw a diameter and label it **d**.
b. Draw a radius and label it **r**.
c. What is the definition of *circumference*? _____
_____

☐ I haven't studied this yet.

25

Use assessment booklet page 25 for question 9.

9. **Use page 25 of the booklet.** Compare your child's answers to the definitions and examples given below. *Check* all **incorrect** answers. *Circle* any problems your child did not attempt to solve.
   a. A diameter passes through the center of a circle and has both endpoints on the circle.
   b. A radius has one endpoint at the center of the circle and one on the circle.
   c. The circumference is the distance around a circle.

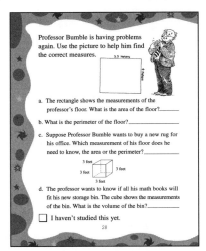

Label each picture. Use the words in the box.

parallel lines	similar polygons	acute angle
right triangle	parallelogram	pentagon
congruent polygons	perpendicular lines	

c. _____   d. _____

e. _____   f. _____

a. _____   b. _____   g. _____   h. _____

☐ I haven't studied this yet.

26   27

Use assessment booklet pages 26 and 27 for question 10.

10. **Use pages 26 and 27 of the booklet.** *Check* all **incorrect** answers. *Circle* any problems your child did not attempt to solve.
   a. right angle
   b. pentagon
   c. parallel lines
   d. congruent polygons
   e. similar polygons
   f. acute angle
   g. perpendicular lines
   h. parallelogram

Professor Bumble is having problems again. Use the picture to help him find the correct measures.

3.5 Meters / 4 meters

a. The rectangle shows the measurements of the professor's floor. What is the area of the floor?_____

b. What is the perimeter of the floor?_____

c. Suppose Professor Bumble wants to buy a new rug for his office. Which measurement of his floor does he need to know, the area or the perimeter?_____

3 feet / 3 feet / 3 feet / 3 feet

d. The professor wants to know if all his math books will fit his new storage bin. The cube shows the measurements of the bin. What is the volume of the bin?_____

☐ I haven't studied this yet.

28

Use assessment booklet page 28 for question 12.

11. **Use page 28 of the booklet.** *Check* all **incorrect** answers. *Circle* any problems your child did not attempt to solve.
   a. 14 square meters
   b. 15 meters
   c. area
   d. 27 cubic feet

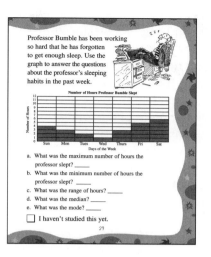

Use assessment booklet page 29 for question 12.

12. **Use page 29 of the booklet.** Can you answer all these questions? Check all that apply.
    a. 6
    b. 1
    c. 5
    d. 3
    e. 3

Use assessment booklet page 30 for question 13.

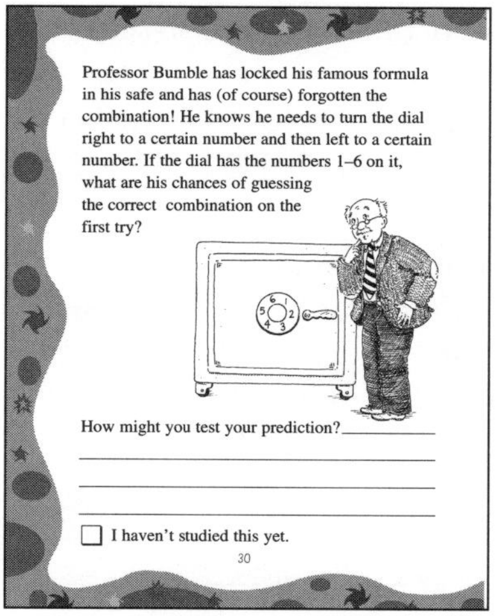

13. *Check* the answer if it is **incorrect.** *Circle* the answer if your child did not attempt to solve the problem. Answer: 1 out of 36. Probability for independent events, such as turning a dial one way and then the other equals the first probability (1 out of 6, or ⅙) times the second probability (⅙): ⅙ x ⅙ = ⅟₃₆.

Ask your child how he or she went about solving the problem. Check all that apply.

___ Read and understood the problem.

___ Came up with a plan for solving the problem.

___ Seemed confident in his or her ability to solve the problem.

___ Used one or more of the following strategies:

    ___ performed an experiment

    ___ drew a picture

    ___ made a chart

    ___ used logical reasoning

___ Persisted until a solution was found.

___ Attempted to solve the problem, but gave up quickly.

___ Did not attempt to solve the problem.

If your child prefers to show you how he or she would test the prediction, you might wish to set aside a block of time for the demonstration. Tests may vary but should include the following:

- A "secret" combination of numbers between 1 and 6 (for example, 2 and 5 or 1 and 3), perhaps chosen by another person.
- A method for randomly picking combinations, such as a spinner, dice, number slips.
- A number of different trials to see how many attempts it takes to pick (toss, spin) the correct combination. The greater the number of trials, the closer the results will be to the actual odds of picking the correct combination.
- A method for keeping track of the results of the trials.

Check one.

___ Did not attempt to devise a test.

___ Test contains none of the elements listed above.

___ Test contains some of the elements listed above.

___ Test contains all of the elements listed above.

Assessment Guide

This assessment guide will tell you what the data you've collected on the Parent Observation form means. It will also direct you to the activity sections in the book that are most appropriate for *your* fifth grader.

Reading and Writing Assessment

Questions 1–3

Ideally, your child read "Dragon Slayer" fluently and with expression. He might have stopped at a word or two, figured them out or guessed at their meaning, and then continued reading. Children who are proficient at reading know that the specific pronunciations of certain words (all those names in a Russian novel, for instance) are less important than the derived meanings from context.

In order to read fluently, your child needs to use a wide range of reading strategies. Relying on a single strategy alone—such as always sounding out words or guessing at the meaning of too many words—will not support your child as he tries to meet the growing challenges of the intermediate school years.

If your child read this passage slowly and haltingly, and stopped at more than nine words, see Struggling Readers, page 95, and Reading Comprehension, page 60. If your child read the passage moderately well, stopped at fewer than nine words, but could use some help in either decoding new words or in developing a greater repertoire of strategies, see Reading Comprehension, page 60, and Vocabulary and Word Study, page 82.

If your child read the passage with ease, stopping at fewer than three words, see Reading and Writing Enrichment, page 122.

Question 4

These questions help you to determine whether or not your child *understands* what he or she reads.

Question A asks your child to identify the genre of the story.

Questions B and C ask your child to identify the problem and solution of the story. To do this, your child needs to recall story events and draw conclusions. The knowledge that stories are frequently structured around a problem and a solution helps students to analyze literature.

Question D determines your child's ability to recognize cause and effect relationships.

Questions E and F assess your child's knowledge of vocabulary or his or her ability to derive the meaning of words from context.

If your child could read the words, but had difficulty answering Questions A, B, C, or D, see Reading Comprehension, page 60, and Writing Exercises, page 98. If your child had difficulty with Questions E and F, see Vocabulary and Word Study, page 82. If your child had difficulty reading most of the words in this story, see Struggling Readers, page 95. (If your child had no difficulty, later questions will direct you to appropriate readings.)

Question 5

Again, these questions will help you to determine how well your fifth grader understands what he or she reads.

Question A asks your child to determine the author's purpose.

Question B asks your child to determine the main idea.

Question C helps you determine your child's ability to distinguish statements of fact from statements of opinion. (If the answer to this question confused *you*, see page 78 for definitions of these kinds of statements.)

Question D encourages your child to draw a conclusion.

Question E determines whether your child understands the meaning of *suffix* and whether or not he or she can identify the suffix in this word.

Question F encourages your child to evaluate the text.

If your child had difficulty with any of the questions from A through D, or

F, see Reading Comprehension, page 60. If your child had difficulty with Question E, see Vocabulary and Word Study, page 82. If your child enjoyed answering these questions, you might want to try some of the activities in Reading and Writing Enrichment, page 122.

Question 6

The ability to collect and organize information is the cornerstone of report writing and oral presentations. Question 6 asks your child to organize information in any way that makes sense to him or her. If you feel your child could use more support in research and study skills, see Study Skills, page 86, and Oral Presentations, page 94.

Question 7

This editing exercise encourages your child to show what he or she knows about spelling, punctuation, and grammar. It is the rare fifth grader who will find all twenty-nine mistakes. But by looking closely at which errors your child found and which were not found, you can pick the most helpful activities to do with your child. Did your child fail to catch the homonyms (there/their, our/are, know/no)? Then see Vocabulary and Word Study, page 82. Did your child miss words that were spelled incorrectly (pant, becuase, froot, etc.) or circle words that were indeed correct? Then see Reading Comprehension, page 60 (the more your child reads, the more he or she will begin to recognize words that "look wrong"). See also Writing Exercises, page 98. Did your child have difficulty recognizing mistakes in punctuation or capital letters? If so, suggest that he or she go back and have a second look with these in mind. If your child still has difficulty recognizing that a question mark should be a period or that a list requires commas, see Writing Exercises, page 98.

If your child could not come up with a synonym for *good,* see Vocabulary and Word Study, page 82.

Question 8

Your goal, of course, is to help your child become the most proficient and prolific reader that he or she can be. If your child is a struggling reader, see Struggling Readers, page 95. If your child *can* read but does not seek books or choose to read regularly, if he or she always waits until the last minute to complete reading assignments, or if he or she groans at the suggestion of reading, see Reading Comprehension, page 60. If your child is already showing the signs of being a lifelong reader, hooray! See the section on Reading and Writing Enrichment, page 122, if you haven't done so already.

Question 9

Knowing where your child is in the process of learning to write will help you respond to written work and support his or her growth as a writer. If you have concerns about any of the questions or the survey your child completed, see Writing Exercises, page 98. To best help your child, you will want to read this section in its entirety. However, know that the questions do correspond with different stages of writing. Here is a breakdown to help you pay closer attention to your child's needs:

Questions A through D inquire about your child's process of *prewriting.*

Questions D through H are intended to look at your child's process of *writing* (there is overlap).

Questions I through J focus on your child's ability to revise.

Questions K through O focus on your child's ability to edit.

Remember, writing and reading skills naturally reinforce one another. Help your child to become a better writer and you will help him or her to become a better reader as well.

Math Assessment

Question 1

Checking for errors in problem solving allows your child to demonstrate his or her understanding of computation methods. If your child had difficulty finding the errors in the problems given but was able to find the correct solutions to the problems, take a few minutes to have him or her explain one or two of the problems to you. Ask how he or she arrived at the correct answer. Your child might simply use a different method of computation. If your child correctly points out the errors but miscalculates the correct answers, ask your child to look over his or her *own* work for errors or to try a second, similar problem. By fifth grade, your child should be able to solve computation problems involving addition, subtraction, multiplication, and division without hesitation. If you feel your child could use more practice in these basic skills, see Number Sense and Whole Number Computation, page 138, and Working Below Grade Level in Math, page 175.

Questions 2–3

By the end of the fifth grade year, your child will be expected to solve computation problems with whole numbers, fractions, decimals, and mixed numbers. Your child's ability to perform these calculations rests on his or her sense of how numbers work, their relative size, their relationships to each other, their equivalent forms, and their properties. In addition, the study of numbers in fifth grade often includes new vocabulary. Numbers are categorized as *primes*, *composites*, *multiples*, or *factors*. A strong number sense will enable your child to be flexible and confident in using a variety of numbers and operations to solve problems. To help your child build a strong sense of numbers and their relationships, see Number Sense and Whole Number Computation, page 138, Problem Solving, page 126, and Functions and Pre-algebra, page 171.

Question 4

Fractions and decimals are the mainstay of most fifth grade math programs. This year, your child will be learning to compare and order fractions and decimals and to compute with both like ($\frac{1}{3} + \frac{1}{3}$) and unlike ($\frac{3}{4} + \frac{3}{8}$) fractions. If your child had difficulty placing $1\frac{1}{4}$, $\frac{1}{2}$, or $\frac{1}{8}$ on the number line, see Fractions, page 144. If your child had difficulty placing 2.25 or .75 on the number line, see Decimals, page 149. If your child answered any of problems a–f incorrectly, see Fractions, page 144.

Question 5

To be successful in math, your child must be able to approach problems with confidence and flexibility. To gain agility in problem solving, your child needs as much experience as possible using a variety of different strategies. If your child could not solve this problem, or to provide additional problem-solving opportunities, turn to Problem Solving, page 126, and Math Enrichment, page 178. If your child chose the wrong operation to solve the problem, see Number Sense and Whole Number Computation, page 138. If your child had difficulty calculating money values, see Decimals, page 149. If your child could not calculate $\frac{1}{3}$ of the total correctly, see Fractions, page 144, and Decimals, page 149.

Question 6

In fifth grade, children extend their understanding of decimal numbers to include addition, subtraction, multiplication, and division of decimals. For additional practice working with decimals, see Decimals, page 149. If your child had difficulty writing a problem, you might wish to provide additional experience in problem-solving strategies and number sense. See Problem Solving, page 126, and Number Sense and Whole Number Computation, page 138.

Question 7

The ability to solve problems successfully requires more than simple skill in calculation. Your child must also learn to approach problems with a sense of inquiry and with logic and persistence. This question provides another opportunity to assess your child's problem-solving skills. Note the behaviors and strategies you checked on the Parent Observation Pages. If you feel that your child could use more practice in solving problems of this sort, see Problem Solving, page 126, and Geometry, page 154.

Question 8

As your child moves out of basic computation and into higher level mathematics, the ability to recognize and create equivalent forms of numbers becomes increasingly important. To move forward in math, your child must be able to move about with ease in the world of fractions, decimals, and percents. This question assesses your child's understanding of basic concepts in all three areas.

If your child answered a incorrectly, see Fractions, page 144.

If your child answered b incorrectly, see Decimals, page 149.

If your child answered c incorrectly, see Ratio and Percent, page 163.

Questions 9–10

This year, your child will extend his or her knowledge of geometry to include the identification and classification of a variety of geometric figures. If your child had difficulty giving examples or definitions of the terms in question 10, or identifying any of the figures shown in question 9, see Geometry, page 154.

Question 11

Most fifth grade teachers assume that their students know how to use standard units to measure length, capacity, weight, mass, and time. By the end of the year, your child will also learn how to solve problems involving area, perimeter, and volume. If your child had difficulty solving any of the problems given, or to give your child additional practice using standard measures, see Measurement, page 159.

Question 12

Most math programs introduce statistical ideas such as mean, median, and mode in fifth grade. To give your child practice in interpreting graphs and statistics, see Probability and Statistics, page 167.

Question 13

Although some children begin studying probability by flipping coins in first grade, others don't touch the subject until fifth or sixth grade. Even if your child has not been introduced to probability concepts, this question will give you a chance to assess his or her creativity and flexibility in solving problems. A child with strong problem-solving skills will generally be able to come up with a reasonable estimation of probability. If your child had difficulty solving this problem or coming up with a plan to test the probability, see Probability and Statistics, page 167, and Problem Solving, page 126.

As you complete the math assessment, remember that no two math programs and no two math teachers are alike. Your child might or might not have been introduced to each of the concepts covered by this assessment. If your child struggled with this assessment, talk to his or her teacher. Ask specific questions about whether your child is working on or below grade level. Read the chapters Working Below Grade Level in Math, page 175, and Working with Your Child's Teacher, page 183, thoroughly and use the other math sections to give your child all the support in math you possibly can. If, on the other hand, your child had little or no difficulty completing this assessment, use this book as a means for enriching your child's understanding and providing opportunities for further exploration. Use the Math Enrichment chapter, page 178, as a jumping-off place, but also skim the rest of the book for activities that catch your or your child's interest. Most of the activities in this book are open-ended so that you can adapt them to be as remedial or challenging as you see fit.

Above all, remember that to succeed in math your child must be confident in his or her own ability to solve problems. Do not underestimate your influence on your child's attitude toward math. If you approach the math that occurs in your daily life with a spirit of inquiry and persistence, chances are much greater that your child will do the same. A positive attitude and comfort with math are the greatest gifts you can give your child.

Reading Exercises

Reading Comprehension

Reading comprehension is absolutely essential for getting good grades in school—in fifth grade and in years beyond. A student must be able to tackle increasingly difficult texts with solid understanding in order to respond to literature, analyze history, solve math problems, follow the instructions to science experiments, assimilate new scientific knowledge, or keep up with homework.

Many parents assume that by fifth grade most children know how to read, that answering questions, completing a book report, or writing a social studies or a science report is more a question of effort, of how much the student tries or applies herself, than a question of reading ability.

On the contrary, reading comprehension is a continually growing skill that affects all other learning and requires constant practice: practice in recalling and organizing information; practice in using thinking skills such as drawing conclusions or summarizing; practice in evaluating what is read and applying the information to their own lives. Children who plateau in reading development in the middle-grade years (grades 4 through 6) will undoubtedly encounter difficulty in completing course work later on.

Simply put, fifth grade is not the time to let go of reading concerns or to cut back on your commitment to your child's reading progress. Even though your child can read on her own, even though her day is filled to the max with obligations and "have-to's," even though your child's teacher has assigned a hefty reading load, take a proactive role in helping your child grow as a reader. Here are three things you can do that will go a long way in supporting your child:

1. Read aloud.
2. Encourage your child to read independently.
3. Help your child develop critical reading skills.

Fortunately, your busy and increasingly social fifth grader still loves stories, and she still loves to talk to her parents. So share good books and stimulating conversation. You will likely learn a great deal about how your child thinks (and find her ability to express abstract thought downright fun). You'll also read some wonderful stories. Most of all, you'll be guiding your child toward future school success.

Read Aloud

Don't you wish there was one thing you could do to ensure your child's happiness? That you could somehow give him solid clues for problem solving or a place to go for the information he needs? That there was a way to help him safely explore the world and develop values that would sustain him through many of life's trials?

Unfortunately, there is no one single thing a parent can do to ensure a child's success. But reading aloud to your child long after the years of pajamas with feet and seven o'clock bedtimes have passed might come pretty close.

Naturally, many parents stop reading to a child who has learned to read on his own. After all, we stop holding on to the end of the bike when riding without training wheels has been mastered, and we stop reminding our child to share when sharing among friends is commonplace. Our job is to help our children learn to do things independently. But so much is relinquished when parents give up the routine of reading aloud to their children.

First of all, modeling is lost. In the same way that budding musicians need to hear good music and budding athletes need to see accomplished athletes in action, growing readers need to hear other capable readers. When you read aloud to your child you introduce words and ideas that, perhaps, he's never heard before. Because you are right there, you can answer your child's questions immediately, helping the new word or knowledge to become as familiar as the slang expressions he picks up at recess.

Choice Read-Alouds for Fifth Graders
- *Crash,* by Jerry Spinelli (Knopf)
- *Grab Hands and Run,* by Frances Temple (Orchard)
- *Journey Home,* by Yoshiko Uchida (Atheneum)
- *The Midnight Fox,* by Betsy Byars (Penguin)
- *One-Eyed Cat,* by Paula Fox (Yearling)
- *Owls in the Family,* by Farley Mowat (Bantam)
- *Phantom Tollbooth,* by Norton Juster (Knopf)
- *Toliver's Secret,* by Esther Wood Brady (Crown)
- *Walk Two Moons,* by Sharon Creech (HarperCollins)
- *Yolanda's Genius,* by Carol Fenner (Aladdin)

Second, children are more influenced by implicit rather than explicit behavior. In other words, they do what their parents do and not what they say. You can tell your fifth grader all the wonderful reasons why you want him to become a good solid reader, but if your child does not see you reading, and genuinely interested in a book on a regular basis, all of these words will be lost.

Third, you can help your fifth grader discover books and authors that he might not find on his own. If he chooses books from the same Hardy Boys or Goosebumps series every time, you can help him discover other books that still meet his interests but challenge his thinking more. There are many outstanding books for middle-grade readers—wonderful stories about genuinely creative people who confront all kinds of difficult problems. If your child is looking for brave heroes who often have to make important decisions, good books offer an endless supply.

But perhaps most important, by reading aloud to your child you will be maintaining a bond that will enrich both of your lives immeasurably. As you talk about the books you read, you will no doubt find out things about your child that you never knew before. Books can offer a window into the quieter places of your child's mind—and yours. By sharing your views on a story plot or a character, you end up sharing your own values and views on the world. Sticky subjects such as peer pressure or sex education—subjects that become difficult to discuss with a self-conscious adolescent—are easier, less loaded subjects now.

Many parents report that reading aloud to their middle grader is one of the best parenting tips they've discovered. Reading aloud helps parents maintain an appropriately close connection to their preadolescents. It allows them to share feelings, important information, and philosophies as a fellow reader. And when sharing good books, there is never a reason to lecture! Whether you've been reading aloud to your child since he was in diapers or you would like to start a new routine of reading aloud now, here are some activities to help.

HAVE FIVE MINUTES?

➤ Read aloud the comics, family horoscopes, a funny quote, or the weather forecast at the breakfast table.

➤ Read aloud a short newspaper article that your fifth grader is bound to find interesting. Articles often provide ways to discuss difficult or complex issues from an objective point of view.

➤ Next time you have a few minutes to spare, read aloud from a poetry collection. Carry a volume of favorite poems (humorous or serious) in your briefcase or in the car, and read from it whenever you have the chance.

You might find that your fifth grader starts to carry a paperback of poetry in her pocket, too!

➤ Identify Genres. It's likely that your fifth grader has outgrown most of the toys in his dentist's or doctor's office. So the next time you're caught waiting, scan a magazine together to determine the different types of writing. In a single magazine, you might find poetry, fiction, editorials, feature articles (nonfiction), advertising, and personal essays. What clues help your child determine the genre?

➤ Reread favorite picture books. Or discover some of the newly published picture books for older children. Many of these picture books introduce important historical or scientific events in a way that fifth graders can readily understand.

HAVE MORE TIME?

➤ Read good books at a regular reading time. It might or might not make sense for you to read every night before your child goes to bed. Other times for reading aloud might be right before dinner, while waiting for siblings to complete an extracurricular activity, or first thing in the morning. If right before bed continues to make the most sense, but your fifth grader covets that time for her independent reading, see if you can't divide the time. You read to your child for the first twenty minutes, then have your child read for a half hour on her own.

➤ Take a moment before or after reading to ask some general questions: "What do you think of this writing?" "Do you like this author's style?" Encourage your child to respond to questions as a fellow reader *and* writer. The more you read, the more you'll notice and be able to talk about literary devices such as point of view or using a wardrobe or a compass to enter a fantasy world. Before long you will feel like "insiders"— members of a reading/writing club.

➤ Read a play to each other. A lively scene such as the tea party in *Alice's Adventures in Wonderland* gives you both an opportunity to ham it up and relax into the roles. Reading a play will also give your fifth grader good practice in reading aloud. Your local librarian can direct you to some appropriate plays for your fifth grader.

➤ Taking a family trip? Bring along some books on tape. Your fifth grader might be interested in listening to *Greek Myths, Arabian Nights, Tales from the Old Testament,* or even *Sherlock Holmes for Children* (all of the above titles were recorded by Jim Weiss). Your local library is likely to have some tape collections for you to borrow. You might even be able to find a story or nonfiction tape about your specific destination.

Encourage Your Child to Read Independently

To develop solid reading comprehension skills, children need practice. Your fifth grader is probably required to do a certain amount of reading at home. It is hoped that she is allowed, at least some of the time, to make her own reading selections. Children, like adults, read with greater enthusiasm, more regularity, and increased attention to detail when they get to read books of their own choosing. If your child's homework does not include independent reading (at least one half hour a day) or if she is not encouraged to choose her own reading material, you will want to find both time and ways to help your child read more.

Some parents report that their child's interest in reading starts to wane during the fifth grade year. This could be due to a number of factors. Fifth graders are increasingly social beings. Whereas the fourth grader is happy to spend some time curled up with a book, the fifth grader can't help wondering what her friends are doing. It's likely that, given a spare moment, she'll hop on her bike or pick up the phone to find out. In addition, there are more demands on a fifth grader's time. If the amount of homework she receives has suddenly tripled from the amount she received last year, she probably resents additional demands on her time.

Realistic Fiction

- *Anastasia Krumpnik* (and others in the collection), by Lois Lowry (Yearling)
- *Arthur for the Very First Time,* by Patricia MacLachlan (HarperCollins)
- *Bad Girls,* by Cynthia Voigt (Scholastic)
- *Bridge to Terabithia* and *The Great Gilly Hopkins,* by Katherine Paterson (Lodestar)
- *The Burning Questions of Bingo Brown* and *The Summer of the Swans,* by Betsy Byars (Viking)
- *Countdown,* by Ben Mikaelsen (Hyperion)
- *Crash,* by Jerry Spinelli (Knopf)
- *Crossing the Starlight Bridge* and *Junebug,* by Alice Mead (Farrar Straus Giroux)
- *Nothing's Fair in Fifth Grade,* by Barthe DeClements (Penguin)

One of the most successful ways a parent can combat these outside influences and help a child to read more is by getting involved as a companion reader. C. S. Lewis once wrote: ". . . a book worth reading only in childhood is not worth reading even then." Fortunately, many editors of children's books know, in the same way that Mr. Lewis did, that exceptional middle-grade fiction appeals to adults as well as children. If you are not familiar with children's literature, ask your local librarian to recommend books that *you* will enjoy, too. Then devote an evening to reading a historical novel, a contemporary story, or a high fantasy. You will be amazed at how easily you become hooked on these tales. Children's literature, which adheres to a stricter sense of story than adult fiction, can be surprisingly satisfying. Share your thoughts about the book you read with your child. By occasionally reading a book that would interest your child, you communicate that reading middle-grade fiction (or nonfiction, if you both have that leaning) is worthwhile. You also build an easy bridge between you and your fifth grader that will likely lead to conversations like this one:

> Mom: I finished *Music of the Dolphins* last night. What did you think of the ending?
>
> Fifth grader: It was a little strange.
>
> Mom: I know what you mean. I think I understand why Nola returned to the sea, but it still left me feeling as if something wasn't entirely resolved.
>
> Fifth grader: That's how I felt. I wanted to know why Nola's father never made an effort to see her. I just kept hoping that he would come and give her a home.
>
> Mom: That's an option that I didn't even think of. But, overall, I loved this book.
>
> Fifth grader: Me, too. Do you know if that author has written any more books?
>
> Mom: I can find out. Maybe we could read another book by Karen Hesse together.

In addition to being a companion reader, try some of these activities to help your reader keep on reading.

HAVE FIVE MINUTES?

➤ Help with transitions. It's hard for anyone, but particularly the busy fifth grader, to slow down and read a book. Help him switch gears by:

- Offering a cup of cocoa or chamomile tea to accompany a good book.
- Suggesting he grab the coveted beanbag chair before anyone else notices that it's available.
- Reading aloud from a new book you just brought home from the library. Read a few pages and hand it off, or sit down and quietly continue the book on your own. Your child will either pick up where you left off or run (having recognized your reading enjoyment) to get the page-turner he's currently involved in.
- Setting a regular family reading time. Many families find that a period before dinner is an ideal quiet reading time.
- Rotating paperbacks in the car. It's hard to resist picking up a book when the lively cover (and marketing experts spend lots of time designing covers to grab unsuspecting fifth graders) is staring up at you.

Historical Fiction

- *Anne of Green Gables*, by L. M. Montgomery (Bantam)
- *The Barn*, by Avi (Avon)
- *Bound for Oregon*, by Jean Van Leuwen (Dial)
- *In the Year of the Boar and Jackie Robinson*, by Betty Bao Lord (HarperCollins)
- *Journey to Jo'burg: A South African Story*, by Beverly Naido (HarperCollins)
- *Jip: His Story*, by Katherine Paterson (Lodestar)
- *Number the Stars*, by Lois Lowry (Yearling)
- *The Printer's Apprentice*, by Stephen Krensky (Delacorte)
- *The Star Fisher*, by Lawrence Yep (Morrow)
- *Runaway Home*, by Patricia McKissack (Scholastic)

• Placing an enticing paperback on the snack shelf. Many of us go to the cupboard when we have an idle moment, and kids are seldom an exception. Imagine your child's surprise when she finds a survival novel next to the microwave popcorn.

➤ Give your child access to the kitchen. He will gain valuable reading practice while following a recipe or the instructions to a chemistry experiment. Be nearby to assist with safety, but refrain from jumping in to explain, demonstrate, or correct. Some of the best learning occurs when the pizza dough won't rise or the cookies burn.

HAVE MORE TIME?

➤ Conduct a reading survey. Who is your child's favorite author? What is his all-time favorite book? What are three things your child loves to do? What are two things he'd like to learn more about? How would he answer this question: Someday I really would like to _____. Take the answers to this survey to your local librarian, who will be thrilled to point out those books or magazines that will please your child. By taking the time to poll your child and find the appropriate books, you will be helping him to see that personal interests can be explored and expanded through books.

➤ Establish a home library and enlist your child as the family librarian. Give him a book allowance and help him choose a selection of paperback books from the bookstore or from his school book club (point out that good libraries carry a *variety* of books). Suggest he pick up books from your local church bazaar, collect old issues of magazines, and establish a place for information downloaded from the Internet. Encourage him to organize the materials in a way that's useful. You might even suggest he construct a lively and comfortable reading corner. As anyone who has ever tried to sort books knows, you can't help but stop the work every now and then and get lost in reading.

➤ Visit the library together often—particularly if your child has a strong interest in nonfiction. Nonfiction books, often accompanied by glorious photographs, charts, or maps, remain in hardcover and are expensive to buy. Plus, there are so many nonfiction topics being published, few bookstores have enough space to meet the interests of everyone. If your local children's

Fantasy and Science Fiction

• *Aliens in the Family,* by Margaret Mahy (Scholastic)
• *The Cat Who Went to Heaven,* by Elizabeth Coatsworth (Macmillan)
• *The Boggart,* by Susan Cooper (Aladdin)
• *The Great Interactive Dream Machine,* by Richard Peck (Dial)
• *Harry the Poisonous Centipede: A Story to Make You Squirm,* by Lynne Reid Banks (Morrow)
• *Mean Margaret,* by Tor Seidler (HarperCollins)
• *The Orphan of Ellis Island,* by Elvira Woodruff (Scholastic)
• *Poppy,* by Avi (Orchard)
• *A Ride on the Red Mare's Back,* by Ursula K. LeGuin (Orchard)
• *Redwall* (and others in the series), by Brian Jacques (Putnam)

librarian knows that your fifth grader loves to read about explorations of Mount Everest, she is more likely to order the newest book on the topic, or at least make a point to mention that it can be ordered through interlibrary loan. (See pages 87–90 for ways to teach your child library skills.)

➤ Suggest that your child read to a younger sibling, cousin, or neighbor. He might even want to volunteer to read a story at the library's story hour. Reading to younger children can be a real confidence booster—not to mention excellent reading practice. For a list of mysteries your child will enjoy, see page 130.

Help Your Child Develop Critical Reading Skills

Did you know that no two people understand written words in exactly the same way? Think back on a time when you were discussing a provocative story with a friend or spouse. Did you agree on the course of events and how they happened? Did you agree on the characters' motives or the emotion that drove the story? Did you agree on the way in which the story ended?

When we differ in our interpretation of stories, we tend to chalk it up to personal opinion. But the truth is, more than opinion is altering the way in which we interpret the words. While we read, we *think* about the story. And how we think about the story depends upon our individual background knowledge as well as our ability to use critical thinking skills such as recognizing cause and effect or drawing conclusions.

Imagine a farmer and an abstract artist reading the directions for running a combine machine. Who will understand more? Now imagine a farmer and an abstract artist reading a book on cubist technique. Who will understand more? Because their prior learning and interests are different, their comprehension of the books is likely to be different, too.

We can't give our children the knowledge to instantly comprehend everything they read. Nor should we, as you can see, insist that they interpret what they read in the exact same way as we do. But we certainly can and should give them the tools and practice for thinking about text.

A person who simply reads the words on a page understands very little. A person who reads the words on that page and thinks about their meaning

Nonfiction

- *Exploring the* Titanic, by Robert Ballard (Scholastic)
- *Growing Up in Coal Country,* by Susan Campbell Bartoletti (Houghton Mifflin)
- *How the White House Really Works,* by George Sullivan (Scholastic)
- *How We Crossed the West: The Adventures of Lewis and Clark,* by Rosalyn Schanzer (National Geographic Society)
- *Immigrant Kids,* by Russell Freedman (Dutton)
- *Protecting Endangered Species at the San Diego Zoo,* by Georgeann Irving (Simon & Schuster)
- *Red Scarf Girl: A Memoir of Cultural Revolution,* by Ji-Li Jiang (HarperCollins)
- *Sea Otter's Rescue: The Aftermath of the Oil Spill,* by Roland Smith (Dutton)
- *Shh! We're Writing the Constitution,* by Jean Fritz (Putnam)
- *Who Really Discovered America?* by Stephen Krensky (Scholastic)

understands more. A person who reads the words, thinks about their meaning, and then goes on to relate their meaning to other learning has understood the most. Here are some very specific skills to help with reading comprehension:

- Identifying the author's purpose.
- Recognizing cause and effect relationships.
- Drawing logical conclusions.
- Making predictions.
- Identifying main idea and details.
- Summarizing.
- Distinguishing fact from opinion.
- Examining graphic aids (charts, graphs, headings).

Identify the Author's Purpose

You've just returned from the mailbox. In your hands are a catalog, three solicitations for money, a memo from your insurance company, an invitation to a party, and an amusing card from your best friend. Which one do you open first? Which pieces of mail do you read slowly, thinking about each word? Which pieces of mail do you skim for just the important information? Which pieces do you toss without opening?

Knowing the author's purpose for each piece of mail in the pile can go a long way toward helping a reader determine *how* to read each piece (slowly with intent to learn, skimming for details, or browsing with a healthy sense of skepticism). Three of the most common reasons authors write are:

1. to inform (the memo from the insurance company, the invitation)
2. to entertain (the card from your friend)
3. to persuade (the solicitations for money)

You'll want to help your child realize, however, that many times an author has more than one reason for writing. The author of the catalog copy, for instance, probably tried to inform, persuade, *and* entertain the reader. As you explore these concepts, you will help your child become a wiser, more discriminating reader.

HAVE FIVE MINUTES?

➤ Headline scanning. Glance over the newspaper headlines with your child. Have her predict what the author's purpose behind headlines such as VOTE TODAY or CAT RESCUES FIREMAN FROM TREE! might be. Choose one interesting article to read aloud. Were her predictions on the mark?

➤ Ask why. The next time your child spontaneously reads the front of a bill-board or the back of a cereal box, ask "Why do you think the author wrote that?" In addition to helping your child think about the purposes of writing, you'll be helping him to realize that writers pen much more than books.

➤ When your child sits down to write a letter, an essay, a report, or a story, ask "What will your purpose for writing this piece be?" And then, "How will you do that?"

➤ Read bumper stickers on your next car ride. Ask your child to determine the authors' purpose of expressions such as "My child is on the honor roll" or "I'd rather be sailing." Suggest that your child make her own bumper sticker using solid-colored contact paper. What is the purpose of her message?

➤ Read a poem or two from a poetry anthology. Can your child see more than one purpose for writing a poem? Might an author have a purpose other than to entertain, persuade, or inform?

HAVE MORE TIME?

➤ Explore stories with morals. For a long time, children's stories were written with one purpose in mind: to teach children proper lessons on living. Aesop's Fables provide children with maxims such as "He who laughs last laughs hardest" and "Not all that glitters is gold." Beatrix Potter's Peter Rabbit stories give a clear indication of what happens to naughty little bunnies (and children). But no book gives lessons so amusingly as Hilaire Belloc's *Cautionary Verses.* Look for a copy in your local library.

Ask your child, "Do you think children's stories are a good way to teach children how to behave? Why or why not? Ask her to determine the author's purpose of her all time favorite book.

Recognize Cause-and-Effect Relationships

Perhaps no skill is more important in comprehension than the recognition of cause and effect. Good story plots follow a taut line of cause and effect. (One event causes another, which in turn causes another . . .) Historical, scientific, and mathematical articles search for and document effects and their causes.

Fifth graders still rely on prompts from parents and teachers to help them identify cause and effect. To help your child identify the cause, ask "Why did this happen?" To identify the effect, ask "What happened?"

Sometimes the cause-and-effect relationship is stated in the text, as with this example: "The gate was locked, so we slipped under the fence." But in other cases your child has to draw his own conclusions. Consider this dialogue:

"Open the gate," said Ted.
"I can't, the gate is locked."
"Good thing we're small," said Ted. Next thing I knew I was on my belly
and under the gate.

You can give your child a real boost toward success if you help him to think about and discuss cause and effect.

HAVE FIVE MINUTES?

➤ What are the consequences? Fifth graders so often concentrate on the present that they sometimes forget to think about cause-and-effect relationships in their own lives. Since it is generally futile during this here-and-now stage to give lectures on what happens when a skateboard is left on the front steps, why not point out transgressions with a more neutral "What do you think could happen if . . . ?"

➤ The next time your fifth grader is happily discussing a series of events that happened at school or on the playground, ask "Why?" "Why do you think Sara is so good at shooting baskets?" "Why do you think Mr. Cromwell made the whole class stay in for recess?" "Why did you decide to go to the library after school today?"

➤ Compose cause-and-effect nursery rhymes (that are clearly more sensible than the original) while driving in the car or waiting for an appointment. Here's one to get you started:

Humpty Dumpty sat on a wall.
Humpty Dumpty had a great fall.
All the king's horses and all the king's men,
Decided to have omelets for dinner.

➤ Play the Midas Touch. Ask your child to imagine that she has a touch that allows her to turn everything to gold—or perhaps to make everything invisible. What are the positive effects of the touch? The negative?

HAVE MORE TIME?

➤ Get involved in your child's favorite cause. Typically, fifth graders have an increased interest in helping to save animals from extinction, in cleaning up ground pollution, or in helping to build a home for a family in need. By volunteering to clean up your neighborhood park or by participating in a walk for Habitat for Humanity, you create wonderful opportunities to talk with your child about personal actions and the effect they will have in the world.

➤ Plant a garden or a window box. Your fifth grader will love the idea of beautifying his own spot of the earth (or growing his own vegetables), and gardening is full of cause-and-effect relationships. What happens if you plant the seeds too deep? What happens if you don't water the plants or if you water the plants too often? What happens if the sun doesn't shine or we have another frost or if the bugs come and are not picked off? Every gardener, no matter how experienced, needs to deal with these cause-and-effect relationships. Don't treat mishaps such as dry plants or chewed leaves as failures. Instead, help your child to think again about causes and effects. What would happen if you put some soapy water on the plant that the bugs love so much?

➤ Suggest that your child write science fiction or fantasy stories. Many children develop a love for these genres during their fifth grade year, and the invention of imaginary worlds calls for cause-and-effect thinking. You might want to help your child prewrite by asking what-if questions such as: "What if there was a world with no colors?" "What if people lived in colonies like ants?" "What if corn kernels were valuable and money was meaningless?"

➤ Play Historical What-Ifs. Ask your child what he thinks would have happened if dinosaurs had not become extinct, if cars had not been invented, if the British had won the Revolutionary War. Encourage him to come up with his own What-ifs and then talk about the effects of each scenario.

Draw Logical Conclusions

Your child already knows how to draw conclusions. Deciding to dress warmly due to overcast skies and determining that she is *not* going to like this evening's casserole because you are soaking beans are fine logical conclusions. What you need to do now is point out how well she draws conclusions in her own life and encourage her to apply this skill to her reading.

Children can be timid about drawing conclusions when it comes to the printed word. The child, who is perfectly capable of inferring all kinds of information in real life, answers questions about the motives of a character or the author's purpose with "I don't know. It doesn't say." Sometimes children need permission to draw their own conclusions (that is, to form their own opinions) about books and articles—especially if they've been led to believe that there is "one right answer" to every question.

We tend to think that the length and sophistication of the words determine the reading level of a book. But reading level is also determined by the degree to which the text calls for the reader to make inferences or draw conclusions. If your child is familiar with all of the words in a story but still doesn't understand it, help her to draw conclusions. Here's how:

HAVE FIVE MINUTES?

➤ Play Silly Conclusions. Begin by making statements such as "This pistachio ice cream is a vegetable. Many vegetables are green; this ice cream is green; therefore, this ice cream must be a vegetable!" Then invite your fifth grader to draw her own silly conclusions. This game will help your child understand that conclusions can be based on logical or illogical reasoning. And as she purposely creates silly conclusions, she'll develop the confidence to create logical ones (a skill she will more readily apply to reading).

➤ Model drawing conclusions when you read together. In addition to telling your child your conclusion, give the information from the text that guided your reasoning.

➤ Ask your child open-ended questions about the book she's reading. Asking questions that don't have a single correct answer—such as "Do you like this character?" "Do you think he did the right thing?" "Do you agree with the author?"—will free your child to give opinions without the added concern of being right. Accept your child's responses with supportive statements such as "Oh, I never thought of that" or "That's good thinking."

HAVE MORE TIME?

➤ Scan the newspaper for items involving crimes. Ask your child to be the judge in the case and come up with a fair punishment. To make this activity more playful, have him come up with a punishment that truly fits the crime. For example, a man who robs a Dunkin' Donuts might be sentenced to eat one hundred and sixty bavarian cream doughnuts a day!

Make Predictions

Just as children draw conclusions, they regularly make predictions throughout their day: "Will Mom let me go to Mark's house after school?" "Will the teacher be mad if I don't finish this math problem?"

Just as making predictions helps your child navigate his way through life, it also helps him navigate his way through a story or a nonfiction article. By constantly predicting, good readers guess what will happen based on their prior knowledge. When the predicted outcome occurs as they expected, their thinking is confirmed. When the predicted outcome is different, they check back or alter their understanding to match the text. While making predictions, readers are actively engaged. The act of predicting gives readers another reason to personally care about what is being read: "Will the character get into trouble as I suspect?" "Will the author tell me, as I predict, that the tiger *can* be saved?"

HAVE FIVE MINUTES?

➤ Post-it predictions. Is your child starting a new book? Together, take a close look at the art on the cover and the description on the back cover or the cover flap. Then, make predictions about the story, write them on Post-it notes (you might want to do this separately), and attach the notes to the inside back cover. After you've completed a few chapters, revise your predictions. When you finish the story, see how close your predictions came.

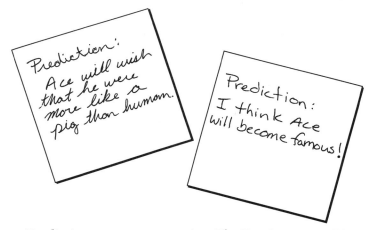

Predictions to accompany *Ace: The Very Important Pig,*
by Dick King-Smith (Knopf)

➤ If you are watching TV, take time during the commercials to make predictions about how the show is going to end. Write several predictions on note cards. Then, based on what you already know, decide which predictions are the most likely to be correct ones.

➤ While reading or talking about fiction, ask questions that help your child identify with the main character and make predictions. What would *you* do if you were the main character?

HAVE MORE TIME?

➤ Read a mystery together. (See page 130 for mysteries fifth graders will enjoy.) Explain, however, that authors who write mysteries deliberately try to mislead the reader. Introduce your child to the term "red herring." The red herring in a mystery is a person who, appearing to be the culprit, draws attention away from the real villain. You and your child might want to keep a chart of clues to help you make and revise your predictions as you read.

➤ Read magazine stories. The stories in children's magazines often have surprise endings. Tell your child that when an author sets out to surprise a reader, she must leave out certain information so the reader *can't* predict the ending. After reading a story with a twist, ask your child to determine what information was missing. Suggest that your child write a story that will surprise his classmates.

Identify Main Idea and Details

Help your child understand that magazine and newspaper articles, reports, and nonfiction essays (such as an encyclopedia entry) have main ideas. This will go a long way toward teaching your child how to organize her thoughts as she reads and tries to recall the information. Focusing on a main idea and supporting details will also give your child skills in writing organized nonfiction.

In third and fourth grade, your child was probably asked to "pick out" the main idea from a nonfiction article. Chances are, the main idea was clearly stated in either the first or the last sentence. At the fifth grade level, children need to learn that the main idea can be implied, rather than succinctly stated in a single sentence. Look at the following paragraph, for instance:

You walk into the cabin and a fire is burning, steaming hot cocoa is on the table waiting for you. In the corner you notice some of your favorite mysteries, in a comfortable chair is a soft blanket and a cat curled up, waiting for your lap.

After reading this paragraph, a child might correctly tell you that the main idea is "the cabin is a really cool place to come in out of the cold." The paragraph *implies* this main idea through use of details. Determining an implied main idea is undeniably a more difficult skill, and it takes fifth graders lots of practice before they learn it. You can help by simply asking "What do you think the author is saying to the reader?" or "What is the most important idea?" Here are some other ways to develop this skill.

➤ Read a brief and interesting newspaper article to your family at the dinner table and have your fifth grader tell you the single most important fact she learned. Encourage your child to tell you the main idea in her own words.

➤ Play What's the Big Idea! While driving in the car or waiting in line at the supermarket, give your child a list of details and have her tell you the main idea of your conversation. For example, you might say "First I had to cut and collect all of the coupons. Then I had to load the bottles we return at the supermarket into the car. Next, I had to make a grocery list. Finally, I arrived at the store to hunt down all of the items on my list." Your child might say that the main idea is that grocery shopping takes many steps—or that it is dreaded work (depending on the tone of your voice).

➤ Talk it out. Fifth graders love to relate the details of their lives to their parents. The next time your child is giving you every detail of a conversation or event, say "So let's see if I have this right. The main idea of what you are telling me is that you think it is unfair that . . ." You don't want to turn every conversation you have with your child into a learning situation, but reflecting back the important points of your child's conversation will give your child a sense of being heard—and understood—and that is a powerful gift to give.

HAVE MORE TIME?

➤ Outline a letter together. Your fifth grader, like many adults, probably loves corresponding with a relative or pen pal but nevertheless puts off the act of writing letters. Often there is *so much* that one wants to say it's hard to get started. To help your fifth grader draft a letter, offer to be her secretary for a moment. Ask her to tell you some of the most important things she would like to tell the recipient. List those major topics, or main ideas, on a sheet of paper with spaces beneath them. Then ask your child to tell you the details of each topic. Many times a single detail will motivate your child to start the communication, and the outline will certainly help keep her going.

Dear Tida,

Main Idea: School ends in one week.
    detail: Been busy putting on the class play and field day.
    detail: Will be sad to leave this school.

Main Idea: Can't wait until you come to visit!
    detail: We can go off the diving board at the town pool this year.
    detail: Sarah Parker's cat is about to have kittens.

Summarize

Students who are taught to summarize what they read have improved comprehension. This might be due to the fact that summarizing requires two important processes: thinking while reading (determining the most important information), and then reorganizing the information into a brief and sensible conclusion.

Make sure your fifth grader understands that summaries are short—no more than a few sentences—and tell only the main ideas of what the story or nonfiction article is about. (If your child is having difficulty determining the main idea of nonfiction articles, do not focus on the skill of summarizing yet. Instead, use more of the activities suggested in the section Identify Main Idea and Details, above.)

HAVE FIVE MINUTES?

➤ At breakfast, ask your child to summarize the events in the story she read last night. Remind her that a summary does not give *every* detail—just the most important ones. (If your child has to do a book summary for school, suggest that she tell the goals of the characters, how they tried to reach them, and whether or not they succeeded.)

➤ Do you have a sports enthusiast in your house? Soccer, basketball, softball, track—whatever season it is, you probably know it as "indigestion season." Meals have to be scheduled around practices and sporting events. You might not be able to get to every game, but you can give your child the chance to tell you what happened. What were the high points? The lows? By recapping the game your child will get much needed practice in summarizing, too.

HAVE MORE TIME?

➤ Whenever you read an interesting article or story, tell your family about it. Include a brief summary. Hearing you summarize will help your child to reorganize his thoughts into a cohesive summary the next time he's called upon to do so.

➤ Webbing. Using a graphic organizer like the one below, known as a web, can be a tremendous help to the fifth grader. Suggest that your child write the title of the story or article in the center of the web. Next, have your child place other important ideas around the center, as shown below. He can use the web to write a summary in paragraph format afterward.

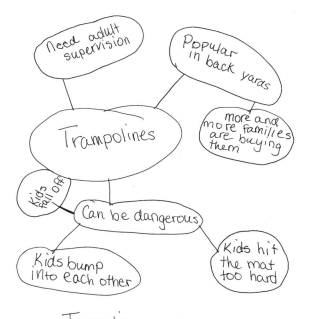

Need adult supervision

Popular in back yards

Trampolines

more and more families are buying them

Kids fall off

Can be dangerous

Kids bump into each other

Kids hit the mat too hard

Trampolines can be fun, but they can be dangerous, too. It's best to have an adult watch.

Distinguish Fact from Opinion

To grow as critical readers—that is, as readers who can distinguish statements of fact from statements of opinion (and thereby develop their own reactions and conclusions)—children need to grow as critical thinkers.

As you work with your child to develop this skill, remember that you are not necessarily trying to teach your child to question the validity of facts but to distinguish between two different kinds of statements. A fact statement can be proven true or false. By reading books, experimenting, or talking to experts, a fact can be documented. "Delaware is the second smallest state" is a statement of fact. So is "The defendant accused the jury of being biased." (If the defendant did say this, then it is a statement of fact.) An opinion, on the other hand, is a judgment and is often preceded by "I believe" or "I think" or is expressed with adjectives such as *beautiful, exciting,* or *rotten.* "Delaware is a charming state" is an opinion. As fifth graders begin to develop this skill they realize (some for the very first time) that you can't believe everything you read.

HAVE FIVE MINUTES?

➤ Next time you're standing in line at the grocery store, read headlines. Which headlines are statements of fact? Which ones state opinions? Which ones blend the two? You might want to point out that the tabloids often write headlines that are statements of fact but mislead readers just the same.

➤ If you don't want to read headlines, read product labels. What does that colorful print on the cereal box say? Are these blurbs statements of fact or opinion? How can you tell?

➤ Give your child a spur-of-the-moment topic and have her give you two statements—one factual and one opinion. For example, the topic might be "fish." Your child's statements might be, "Cod fish are larger than guppies" (fact) and "Fish have the ugliest-looking eyeballs" (opinion).

➤ "Eddie Maker says . . ." Ah. How many times have you heard "facts" attributed to such reliable experts as the leading fifth grade actor or the playground bully? The next time you hear one of these authorities quoted by your fifth grader, take a minute to help your child examine the nature of the statement (not the source). Ask: "Do you think that Eddie's statement—'Boys have the most awesome ideas'—is a statement of fact or opinion?"

➤ Play a game of Telephone. We never outgrow this game, which is a classic way to see how facts can be distorted. A group forms a circle. Someone whispers a fact statement in the next person's ear. He, in turn, passes it on. Each time, a participant receives a statement, determines to the best of his or her ability what was said, and then passes it on to the next ear. Help your child notice how the introduction of emotion-packed words such as *smelly* changes the entire tone and meaning of a message. See how the rumors run!

Examine Graphic Aids

Authors and publishers know that some information can be provided more efficiently with a picture than with a lengthy string of words. For instance, webbing is a process that is far easier to show than describe (see the web on page 77). Unless students are shown how to read graphic aids, however, they might miss crucial data.

For some people, particularly visual learners, graphic aids are rather self-explanatory. But for other types of learners, such as auditory or kinesthetic learners (learners who need to move or to "do" to know), visual aids are one more difficult code to crack. And all children, visual or otherwise, need to be introduced to how things such as pull-outs, legends, and timetables work. Take the time to explore graphic aids with your child.

Here are some samples of graphics your child might come across in his reading.

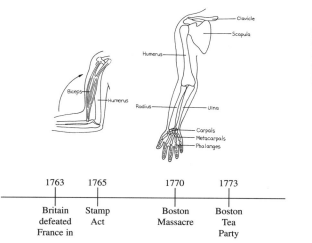

HAVE FIVE MINUTES?

➤ Take five minutes next time you're at the library and skim some nonfiction books. Which books appear to be better organized? Which books seem easier to read? Which look as if they'd have more interesting information? Why? Talk to your child about the photographs, boxes, headings, and captions. How do these added details help the reader? Tell him that he will better understand what he is reading if he takes the time to explore these aids.

➤ Observe your child the next time he is playing with a computer game or visiting the Internet. No doubt he is looking at a graphic aid on the screen. Ask him to describe the aid (be it a graph, diagram, or map) and how it works. This will give you an opportunity to correct any misconceptions your child might have or to add to his knowledge.

➤ Point out graphic aids such as a weather chart, a graph, or photograph captions in the newspaper. If your child has an avid passion for business, sports, or fashion, she might want to collect graphics from the newspaper to paste in a scrapbook.

HAVE MORE TIME?

➤ Take time to read nonfiction together. If your first thought about nonfiction is that it means dry, boring textbooks, you're in for a treat. Nonfiction for children has had a boom time; books explode with engaging information presented in intriguing formats. Some of the most recent nonfiction reads like a suspense story (see the box on page 67 for recommendations). As you pore over these beautiful books, show your child how to use the graphics. In fact, you might explore the graphics in a book one night and then read the text together the next. The information you glean from the graphics will act as background information, helping your child understand more of what she hears.

➤ To reinforce the advantages of graphics, have your child make her own when the need arises. Here are some ideas that might be helpful:
  • a map (complete with map key) of the route she takes to get to a friend's house
  • a diagram of a birdhouse or lemonade stand she built from scratch
  • a table of sports statistics comparing her favorite players or teams
  • a timeline demonstrating the most meaningful events in her life so far
  • a bar graph comparing family members' favorite vegetables, TV shows, or Beanie Babies

- a scale drawing of her room, fort, or clubhouse
- a schedule of her daily events—or a carpool timetable for you!

➤Use graphics to make family life easier. Set up a family bulletin board and post charts, graphs, and visual reminders. Here's a graphic aid to get you started:

- Revolving chore chart. Take a sheet of poster board and cut out a circle six to eight inches in diameter, larger if you prefer. Cut another about an inch wider. Divide the smaller circle into pie pieces, one for each family member. On the outer circle, write the daily or weekly jobs that need to be done. You can double up on some of the easier ones in order to get a number to match the number of family members. Push a brad fastener through the center of both circles, placing the smaller one on top (a pushpin on a bulletin board works, too). Each day or week, ask your child to rotate the chart. He can take a chance and spin it, or advance it methodically one space to the right or left. Allow family members to swap duties if they wish.

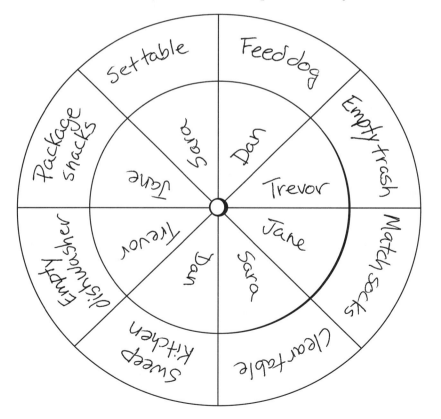

Vocabulary and Word Study

While your child was learning to read, she was exposed to books with controlled vocabularies. Reading textbooks have carefully chosen words. Even children's chapter books are often written for specific grade levels, which means that the author has paid some attention to the difficulty of the words. But now that your child has reached fifth grade, she is no doubt presented with more sophisticated fiction, often chosen to accompany the social studies curriculum, as well as challenging nonfiction. She will read science and math texts with highly specific words. In order to continue to succeed in school, your child's vocabulary must keep pace with the increasing demands of these reading texts.

Vocabulary work in school, which usually requires a child to look up words in the dictionary in order to complete worksheets or workbooks, can be downright dull. But word study at home (where real strides in language development occur) can be a natural process of learning together. In fact, the most favorable activities for vocabulary development are probably two that you are doing already—reading to and talking to your child. Young children love to explore and play with words. There is no reason why a ten- or eleven-year-old child need stop.

Children who acquire a command over words not only succeed in school, they are better equipped for life. With the right word, your child can write precisely, read thoughtfully, speak eloquently. With the right word, your child can persuade, inform, entertain, or inspire. Here are some ways to find joy in words.

HAVE FIVE MINUTES?

➤ Word origins. Words are constantly changing. Did you know that the word *speed* originally meant "success" and "good fortune"? When someone set out on a journey, he was wished "Godspeed!" Or did you know that the word *nice* originally meant "ignorant"? Word scholars suspect that it went from meaning "ignorant," to "shy," to describing someone who could judge fine things, and eventually came around to referring to someone who is agreeable. Look for a dictionary of word and phrase origins. Take turns presenting a word and its origin at the dinner table. Or post a word and its origin on your family bulletin board.

➤ Write up menu ideas for the week. Post them on the refrigerator and ask your child to write an adjective (*delicious, scrumptious, disgusting*) beside each item to describe how she feels about it.

➤ Keep a running list of words on the refrigerator. Take turns choosing a category—such as color words, synonyms for *talk* (*chat, discuss, converse*), or homonyms (*there, their,* and *they're; blue* and *blew*). Throughout the week encourage family members to record words that fit the category. This is a great way for busy families to feel connected. As your fifth grader goes to the refrigerator to record *cobalt blue,* she will see that Dad thought of *beige,* her little sister thought of *white,* and Mom just added *vermilion.* Even if the word *vermilion* sends her running to the dictionary, she'll feel like a team player. At the end of the week, read the amazing list of words your family generated.

➤ Use synonyms (words that mean almost the same thing) in your daily talk. If your fifth grader tells you that math class is boring, reflect back to what she said using another word for *boring.* Your conversation might go something like this:

> Child: Math class is so boring!
> Dad: You think math class is dull?
> Child: Well, it's not exactly dull. Sometimes the teacher gives us cool problems, but it's so long.
> Dad: It's unreasonably extended.
> Child: Well, I just don't know what to do. I don't really get the math.
> Dad: Do you find the math hard?
> Child: I guess so. I really don't understand what I'm supposed to be doing.

As you can see from the example, reflecting back with more precise words will not only introduce new vocabulary, it will help your fifth grader clarify her thoughts. By helping the child to be more accurate, this father got to the crux of the *real* problem.

➤ Play Multiple Meanings. One of you chooses a word such as *case.* Others use the word in a sentence, each sentence demonstrating a different meaning for the word: He carried a brief*case* to work; She had a big *case* coming up in court tomorrow; She bought a *case* of grapefruit; "Get off my *case!*" he shouted. Both the one choosing the word and the one coming up with sentences stretches some of those word muscles.

➤ Dissect words. When your child asks you what a word means, you have a variety of options for your response. You can send her to the dictionary. You can

Don't be afraid to use "big words" with your child. You will be amazed at the words she can understand if you use them in context. And fear not. By using longer words (as long as they're more precise) you will not be teaching your child to be pretentious. Instead, you will be giving her choices. As more than one mother has been heard to say, only those with small vocabularies need to use inappropriate (that is, profane) words.

tell her the meaning. Or you can help your child take apart the word to sleuth out its meaning. Often there will be a prefix (such as *un-* in *unimaginable*) or a prefix (such as *-able* in *unimaginable*) that holds clues. Show your child how to break the word into syllables and tell you what she knows about them. Share what you know, too: "I see the root word *imagine* in the middle here. I know that *un* means 'not,' and *able* means, well, 'able.' So *unimaginable* means 'unable to imagine.'" This is a skill that will stand your child in good stead, not just in reading but in standardized test taking as well.

HAVE MORE TIME?

➤ Eat together. A family that protects mealtime as time spent together without the distractions of radio or television will find that wide-ranging discussions can result. Talk about the day's events, family concerns, or politics, and share a good joke. Communication is by far the best vocabulary builder.

➤ Build words together. Make your own set of magnetic word parts from magnetic tape and labels (magnetic tape can be found at your local hardware store). Place prefixes, suffixes, and root words on the refrigerator and challenge your child to see how many words she can make—and tell you the meaning of! (Post a list so she can use the same word parts over and over again.) Here is a list of prefixes and suffixes to get you started. Use your dictionary to choose base words.

Prefixes	**Suffixes**
pre- (before)	-ly (in the manner of)
re- (again)	-ful (full of)
mis- (badly, wrongly)	-less (without, lacking)
un- (to reverse)	-er (one who)
ir- (not)	-ive (have or tend to be)
im- (not)	-al (of, like, or suitable for)
dis- (apart)	-ous (having the qualities of)

➤ Color associations. Ask your child to select a marker. Then have her list everything she can think of that the color of the marker reminds her of. You might want to suggest that she make a web with the categories, such as "things," "feelings," "words." This will help her to think beyond traditional word associations.

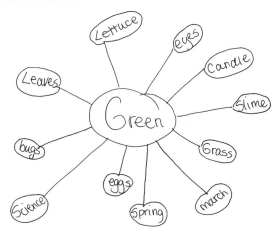

➤ Play Fictionary. This game requires three or more players and a dictionary.

FICTIONARY

1. One player chooses an unknown word from the dictionary.
2. Other players write a mock definition on slips of paper, using dictionary style, while the player who chose the word copies down the real definition (just one meaning).
3. The player who knows the real definition reads all of the responses.
4. All players try to guess which definition is the correct one. Players get a point for choosing the correct definition. The player who chose the word gets a point each time another player chooses a wrong definition.

➤ Play Charades. You can choose words that appear in your child's homework or words that relate to subjects, such as the American Revolution, that she's studying in school. While playing Charades, it is likely that your fifth grader will explore both the context of words and word parts.

➤ Collect idioms. Idioms (more commonly known as expressions) are several words that, when put together, create a whole new meaning. See how many idioms your family can come up with on your next family vacation or long car ride. Here are a few to start you off:

- foot the bill
- miss the boat
- bouncing off the walls
- over my head
- hit it off
- in the dark
- up in the air
- down in the dumps

➤ Challenge your child to write a humorous picture book using idioms. Suggest, however, that she illustrate the story with literal translations like the one on the opposite page.

Make sure your fifth grader has a good understanding of the skills introduced in earlier grades. Without these skills, your child will undoubtedly experience frustration when working independently.

- How to use a dictionary (alphabetical order, guide words, pronunciation key, multiple meanings, sentence context).
- How to use a card catalog (manual or computer).
- The difference between fiction and nonfiction.
- How to find nonfiction books using the Dewey decimal or Library of Congress system.
- How to use the different parts of a book (table of contents, index, glossary).

Study Skills

Many parents report that their fifth graders are suddenly bombarded with homework, long-term assignments, and organizational challenges. It seems as if fifth grade is the year to acknowledge that your child is no longer in primary school and increased responsibility is in order. Whether or not fifth grade is the appropriate year to increase expectations of independent study work is not certain. But what is certain is this: Your child will need your help in order to prioritize, schedule, and complete multistep projects successfully. You can begin by focusing on these four areas:

1. Planning ahead.
2. Organizing information.
3. Test-taking skills.
4. Giving oral presentations.

Every moment you can spend helping your child develop good study habits and good study skills at this stage will help prevent years of agony over last-minute reports (called "Sunday night specials" by teachers), late or incomplete homework, and failed tests.

My brother is driving me up the wall.

Planning ahead

HAVE FIVE MINUTES?

➤ If your child's school doesn't provide an assignment calendar for your child, buy or make one. Show him how to break an assignment into smaller chunks and record the steps on the calendar. For instance, if your child has one week to write a report, suggest that he record "Choose a topic" on Monday. On Tuesday, he might write "Find information." On Thursday, "Begin taking notes." When thinking about a project, students often think only of the final product, which leads them to believe that they can get that report done on the weekend. By helping your child plan ahead, you will help him remember that writing a report involves much more than writing.

Help your child to find a productive place to study. This can be in a corner of the den or kitchen, as most children prefer not to be isolated during homework time and benefit from a parent's presence. And go ahead and let your child listen to music if she wishes. Listening to music, particularly baroque music, can help children relax and learn. Allowing your child to make her own selections will help her feel more responsible for her studies, and with the teen years fast approaching, this is an important goal.

➤ If your child has a book report due, have him record the number of pages he needs to read each night in order to have completed the book in time to write the report or plan the presentation.

➤ Brainstorm sources of information each time your child begins a new project. We all tend to think of encyclopedias and nonfiction books, but what about magazine articles, talking with local experts, the Internet, and historical fiction to help your child develop a better understanding and therefore "hooks" for the information, songs, or epic poems to add vitality? Look at the list of possible sources a fifth grader came up with for a report on birds.

Brainstorming sources at the beginning of a project will also help your child determine whether or not he chose a workable topic.

Audubon Society
Mrs. Eaton (birdwatcher)
A field guide to Birds
SIM Park Software (birdcalls)
The Bird atlas
Bird Watching for kids
Bird watch (poetry)
InterNest (website)
Kids Korner Birds (website)

➤Explore a different reference book or a computer reference source each time you visit the library. A library's reference section is still pretty awesome and mysterious for most fifth graders. Sure, they can pick out the encyclopedias and the dictionary, but what are all those other books and why would anyone want to read them? Begin with a "cool" book like the *Guinness Book of World Records*. No child can resist the illustrations of a 53-inch-long thumbnail or a 22-foot-long earthworm. From the book of records, move on to the almanacs. These are books with facts on everything from what year the X ray was invented to how the state of Kansas got its name. See if your child can find out the population of your closest city or the population of a country she'd like to visit. On subsequent visits, check out the special dictionaries. Perhaps your library has a biographical (who would your child like to know more about?) or a geographical dictionary (what does the dictionary say about your town?). And don't forget the atlases! Ask the librarian to show you sources, such as CDs, that you might not be familiar with.

HAVE MORE TIME?

➤Take turns picking a place that you would like to visit someday. Write down what you think or recall about the place. Then, on your next library visit, investigate the geography of that location. One family, who thought they would like to go to Peru because of the warm sandy beaches, was startled to find out that Peru has penguins on its rocky coast! This activity will give your child lots of practice in reading maps and locating important information.

➤Use reference works to solve crossword and other word puzzles together. Using reference books isn't cheating. It's learning. What is a city in Portugal that begins with *L*? Use an encyclopedia or atlas. What is another word for *evil*? Use a dictionary or thesaurus. Who won the Academy Award for best actress in 1998? Check an almanac.

Organizing Information

Once your child has established a topic, he's presented with the incredible task of gleaning and organizing the information. This is not an easy task for anyone, let alone a fifth grader who would much rather be outside playing. To help him practice these skills and get the job done, make the task of organizing information as much fun as possible. Start by purchasing a few tools: high-lighters, Post-it notes, index cards, and a new notebook are fairly inexpensive but go a long way toward motivating a child to get down to business. Next, try to be present while your child is collecting and organizing information. You can suggest activities to help (see the list below) and answer questions as they arise. By being near, you can give your child that occasional nudge that says, I know you can do this, and once you've learned how, you'll have this tool always.

HAVE FIVE MINUTES?

➤ Are you going to miss a favorite family TV show? Ask your child to take notes! Explain to your child that taking notes is a way of remembering what you heard or read. When you write notes, you record only key words or the most important facts (main ideas). Later, ask your child to tell you all about the TV show while using his notes to guide him.

➤ Leave your child notes that contain only key words: "Doing errands. Back 4:40. Let Daisy out. Love You." Modeling this kind of note taking will help your child be brief when taking research notes.

➤ Buy multicolored note cards. Suggest that your child use one color to record notes for each part (subtopic) of his report. For instance, when writing a report about the respiratory system, he could record facts about body organs on pink cards, facts about the breathing process on yellow cards, and facts about pollution and lung diseases on blue cards. Help him decide how to order the report once he has completed his note taking. Remind him that some of the information on the cards might be irrelevant.

➤ Play Tell Me the News. If your child brings home a weekly newspaper (published by Scholastic or Weekly Reader) or a newsletter from his teacher or principal, ask him to read the paper and then *tell* you the news. Having him tell you the news instead of reading it aloud will give him good practice in paraphrasing—an important step in reorganizing infor-mation.

➤ Webbing. It is likely that your child has learned this organizational tech-nique in school. Begin by writing a main idea at the center of a sheet of paper. Circle it. Draw lines to record secondary ideas, then circle them. On the opposite page is a web one fifth grader made to record informa-tion about the Oregon Trail.

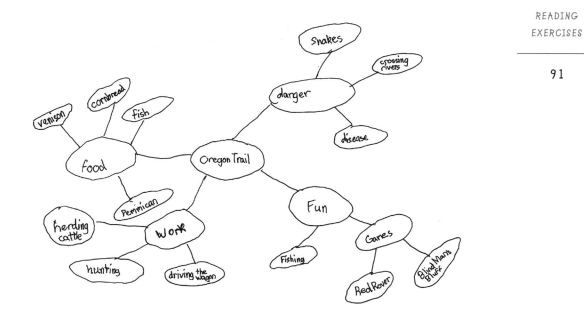

➤ Encourage your child to take a look at the newspaper every day. Suggest that he scan the paper for interesting articles to read. Scanning is an important skill in locating information and developing an understanding of how books are organized.

➤ Allow your child to browse the magazines at supermarket checkout counters. Finding information about a favorite movie star or athlete will give your child much needed practice in scanning and skimming (see the activity below for definitions of these two skills).

HAVE MORE TIME?

➤ Bake a dessert together. What does cooking have to do with study skills? The process of finding and following a recipe can help teach your child to skim and scan.

Imagine looking for a recipe and reading every word of every recipe until you found the one that pleased you. It could take you days! Instead, you **scan** the cookbook (look it over quickly, moving from one point to another) for a recipe that fits the bill. When you find a likely candidate, you **skim** the recipe (read or glance through it quickly) to see if you have all the ingredients or the necessary time and equipment. Suggest that your child find a recipe he would like to make. Be sure to make the connection between the process of looking in a cookbook and the process of looking for information. You might say, "When you're looking for information on the clothing worn during colonial times, you can search history books in the same way. First you scan for the colonial period, then you skim that information for the word *clothing*, or other key words." As your child follows the recipe while cooking, his eyes will skim the page over and over again.

➤Outline your next family outing or get-together. Teaching your child how to outline while also learning academic information combines two difficult skills. Instead, outline a day in the city, a camping trip, or Gramps's birthday party. In case it's been a long time since you wrote an outline, here is an example to follow.

Take time to listen to your child. This might seem obvious, but sometimes schedules get hectic and we don't always remember to give our children air time—time to inform, time to entertain, time to engage in a philosophical debate. A child who grows up comfortable communicating at home will have an easier time dealing with the demands of an oral presentation.

Carnival Party Materials

I. Games
  A. Bean Bag Toss
    1. bean bags
    2. backboard
    3. paint
  B. Sponge Throw
    1. sponges
    2. water
    3. backdrop
    4. paint
    5. Dad
  C. Miniature Golf
    1. blocks
    2. tin cans
    3. golf balls
    4. golf clubs
  D. Face Painting
    1. face paint
    2. table
    3. brushes
    4. water

II. Food
  A. Cake
  B. Ice Cream
  C. Punch
  D. Cotton candy

Test-Taking Skills

Don't forget to study! These are words children often hear as they race out of the classroom at the end of the day. But what do these words mean to a fifth grader? Very little sometimes. Even children who have had weekly spelling tests for the past three years might not know what it means to study. Do you stare at the words for a long time? Do you read the words over and over and see how much you remember? Just how do you study?

Here are some helpful study tips.

1. Help your child make a list of categories or vocabulary that she thinks will be on the test. Encourage her to look over chapters of textbooks, worksheets, and any other material she has been using to study the subject. If she is unable to begin, suggest she record the headings in her textbook. Chances are, the material on the test will be categorized in the same way.

2. Have her tell you the most important facts and concepts, in her own words, under each category. If she can't recall the facts, suggest she use the categories to make a web, and record what she needs to know on the web (see page 91 for an example of how to make a web). As your child records information, try to help her relate the information to her own life. You might say something such as, "Remember when Alison rejoined your club after being away for a long time? She decided that she would be president again. Most of the club members were upset by that decision. Perhaps that's how the colonists felt when Britain began to govern the colonies again."

3. Question your child about the things she's learning: "Why do you think the colonists did that?" "Why do you think this information is included in this book?"

4. Talk about ways to memorize difficult words or facts. Acronyms are often helpful. For remembering the notes that go with the lines of a musical staff, for instance, your child could memorize: **E**very **G**ood **B**oy **D**eserves **F**udge. Making up a song about important information can help: "The sixteen counties of our state are . . ." So can associations: **D** is for **D**own as in **D**enominator.

5. Using the list she made in Step 1, have your child test herself the night before the real quiz. Or have her respond to your questions. As your child grows older, she'll be able to ask study friends to do the same for her.

Oral Presentations

Schools and teachers vary in their expectations of children and oral presentations. By fifth grade your child might have given numerous oral reports and recitations, or perhaps he is facing the prospect of standing up in front of the class for the very first time. In either case, you might want to skim the activities suggested below. Giving good oral presentations is a skill that evolves slowly and requires much practice. Simple techniques can give the beginner confidence and the natural performer a new trick or two.

HAVE FIVE MINUTES?

➤ Give your child lots of practice speaking in front of others. Grandma is turning sixty-five? A cousin is turning sixteen? Encourage your child to pick or write a special poem to recite at the birthday event. If appropriate, suggest that your child include a poem or quote in her school presentation.

➤ Invite your child, alone or with others, to lip-sync her favorite song. Urge her to dress the part and ham it up. Take a few moments to be an appreciative audience, whether you care for rap or not. Remember that by performing in this way she's gaining experience in stage presence.

➤ Tell jokes. Many professional speakers know that a joke can relax the audience—and subsequently the speaker. And those who welcome laughter will not become unnerved if something goes wrong during the presentation. In fact, tell your child that many speakers welcome silly mistakes because it gives the audience and the speaker time to laugh together.

➤ Help your fifth grader organize his presentation. If he is going to give a book report, you might want to suggest that he complete one of the graphic organizers on pages 201–4 in the back of this book. If it is a science or social studies presentation, suggest he use props such as magazine pictures, charts, maps, or actual objects to keep himself on track during his presentation. He can place his props in a particular order and use them to guide his thinking and speaking.

➤ Keep an eye out for extracurricular programs such as Odyssey of the Mind, chorus, or drama club. Children who participate in these activities grow more comfortable performing in front of groups.

➤ Fund drives. Is your child being asked to sell candy bars, gift wrap, or grapefruit again? Although it might be easier for you to bring the order form in to work, encouraging your child to make the phone calls or go door-to-door (don't forget to set safety parameters) can provide valuable training in oral presentation.

HAVE MORE TIME?

➤ Encourage your child to rehearse her presentation in front of a home audience. Talk to her about the ABCDE's of speech making: **A**ttitude, **B**ody language, **C**larity (of material), **D**iction, and **E**xpression. If possible, ask her if she would like you to videotape her presentation so she can self-edit. Or gently parody bad speeches.

➤ Tell stories. Storytelling is perfect practice for public speaking. A properly told story demands that its teller keep the main idea of the story in mind, organize the story's sequence and details, and look for ways to keep the audience engaged. Fables, myths, folktales, and fairy tales all make excellent storytelling fare.

➤ Attend plays and other performances. Discuss the quality of the shows. Could your child hear everything the actors said? Did they speak with expression? What impressed your child most?

Struggling Readers

Children who are below grade level in reading are often referred to by educators as "reluctant readers." By fifth grade, children who have not begun to read with considerable fluency might *appear* to be reluctant. They probably groan when assigned reading skill work or research that requires reading. They likely avoid reading aloud or answering comprehension questions in class. No doubt they choose the thinnest books with the fewest number of words per page and, yes, will even fake reading.

But reluctant? Hardly. No one would choose the plight of the poor performing reader. Struggling to decode words, to make sense of multisyllabic words, to create meaning from print is hard and often embarrassing work. No, the term "struggling reader" better defines these children.

Fifth graders who are stumbling, reading word by painful word, desperately need your assistance. First of all, they need you to be their advocate. If your child has not been identified as needing additional reading support and/or special school services, talk to her teacher. Suggest that your child be tested for any problems, such as a learning disability, that might be getting in the way of her reading.

Second, you must create a safe and supportive reading environment at home. Poor readers need two things: one-to-one support, and lots of time spent actually reading. They do not need more time with flashcards or completing skill workbooks. You are in the best position to provide both of these requirements. Tell your fifth grade child that it is not too late for her to grow into a capable and confident reader and that you will help her. Here are some ways to begin.

- Establish a time when you and your child can read together each day. Do not use this time as punishment by saying things like "Until you get your grades up, we're going to sit here and read" or take it away as a reward: "If you clean your room today, you can skip reading time." Practice reading in the same nurturing and supportive way that you might help your child learn to make a grilled cheese sandwich or catch a baseball. Approach each session in a positive, you-can-do-it way.
- Take turns reading aloud. When it is your fifth grader's turn, try not to make her feel as if she's being tested. If she stumbles over a word, you might say, "I often stumble over words like that, too." If she comes to a word she doesn't know, you can ask, "What would make sense here?" or "What letter sounds do you recognize?" and then encourage her to keep going. Simply provide some words now and then to help your child keep momentum.
- Find books your child can read successfully *and* that meet her interests. Help her find stories about kids she can relate to. Your librarian will be your best resource. Remember that home is the place your child can practice reading without comparing page length, print size, or oral fluency with classmates. Don't let her label books as "baby books." Encourage her to read anything that catches her fancy and will help her feel successful.
- Until your child is reading beginning chapter books, sit down with more than one book at a time. If your child experiences success with one book, she'll probably want to start another immediately. Don't lose this perfect opportunity.
- Make reading a social event in your home. If you pressure your child to read—but everyone else is watching TV, talking on the telephone, or playing games—she'll feel isolated. Read with and beside your child. Share interesting facts or fun lines. Sigh when you get to the good parts.
- Talk to your child. Let her know that you recognize her struggle and her efforts and that you have begun to search for ways to help her. By acknowledging and accepting her difficulties, you might be able to prevent her from "faking it" as a reader. Let her know that many famous

people such as Leonardo da Vinci, Thomas Edison, and Albert Einstein had reading problems. (And if that doesn't make an impression, how about Tom Cruise, Magic Johnson, and Whoopi Goldberg?)

- Children in the fifth grade find themselves reading more than one book at a time. They might read one book during formal reading time, another during independent reading time, another for social studies, and yet another at home. This can be defeating for the emergent reader who is just learning to follow a story or stay involved in chapter books. If this is the case, ask your child's teacher if your child can stick with one book until completion. Suggest that she carry the book back and forth from school.

- Watch a movie with your child and then suggest she read the same story in book form. (Look for those that say "Movie tie-in"; they have been written to closely follow the visual presentation.) The movie will provide her with knowledge of the setting, characters, and plot—a tremendous boost for the struggling reader.

- Consider hiring a well-trained reading tutor or finding a school volunteer who can help. The right person or program can often launch the struggling reader.

- Be careful not to verbally blame your child's school or her teacher. Once you've begun to communicate that you value your child's education, you have begun to give her permission to do the same. Work with the school in any way possible and continue to show your child that her education matters.

For support and ideas, see some of the books listed below. Your library might have many more resources not listed here.

- *Solving Your Child's Reading Problems*, by Ricki Linksman (Citadel Press)
- *Unicorns are Real*, by Barbara Meister Vitale (Warner)
- *Unlocking Your Child's Learning Potential*, by Cheri Fuller (Pinon)
- *Keys to Parenting a Child with a Learning Disability*, by Barry E. McNamara and Francine J. McNamara (Barrons)
- *Parenting a Child with a Learning Disability: A Practical, Empathetic Guide*, by Cheryl Gerson Tuttle and Penny Paquette (Lowell House)
- *Taming the Dragons: Real Help for School Problems*, by Susan Setley (Starfish)

Writing Exercises

The process of writing is often oversimplified. When you were in school, you probably sat down to write a paper the day before it was due. At school, you handed it in and waited for the teacher's comments, which usually came in the form of red marks all over your paper. It is hoped that the teacher commented on your voice and what you had to say; more likely, she commented on the spelling and grammatical errors she hoped you would correct next time. The majority of students came away with the devastating impression that they couldn't write, that there wouldn't be a next time if they could help it.

In recent decades, teachers have taken a much closer look at how to support writers in the classroom. They know that a student's voice must be encouraged and that the message needs time to develop and change before the mechanics of writing should be focused on. Educators recognize that there are four stages to writing: prewriting, writing, revision, and editing. However, even this model is too simplistic. Writers do not pass through these stages in a straight, sequential line. Instead, they spiral through them: "Prewriting, on to writing, revising that line . . . Whoops! This idea won't work. Back to prewriting."

You will see that the recommended activities in this book have been divided into the four stages of writing to help you develop a better understanding of their importance. However, many of the activities listed under one category, such as writing, would also serve well as prewriting exercises or even as revision activities. The key is to help your child see that writing is more than putting marks on a paper and waiting for the teacher's comments. Writing is finding what you want to say and saying it the best way you know how. Sometimes that involves play, sometimes that involves questioning yourself and others, sometimes that involves going through the piece with your own editor's pen.

Prewriting

Ask any professional writer to describe moments of fear and frustration and you're bound to hear of the terror of facing the blank page. Beginning a new piece of writing can be extremely difficult for beginners and professionals alike. If your fifth grader procrastinates when it comes to writing projects, if he's willing to clean his room rather than put pencil to page, he probably has not spent enough time prewriting.

Prewriting is not a luxury—it is an essential part of the writing process. Prewriting allows the writer to explore topics (not every idea is a successful idea). It gives him time to work with organization before committing words to paper and can save revision time later. But, perhaps most important, knowing what he wants to write and having a few good ideas can give him tremendous confidence—just the thing that's needed to begin. Children, who do not get enough time to prewrite, often experience frustration and a debilitating sense of not being effective as writers.

Talk it out. Many children (and adults!) rehearse writing by talking out loud. Encourage your child to tell you his story or information for his report. As he talks, he will begin to recognize parts that need clarifying or sections that require more information. You can provide a nudge here or there by asking a sincere question, but be careful not to impose your thoughts on the project. Rehearsal is a fragile time, and you want your fifth grader to know that he doesn't need to look to others for good ideas.

HAVE FIVE MINUTES?

➤ Suggest that your child begin a project by finding a special place and letting his mind wander. That's right! Let your child sit and daydream. Daydreaming, or mind spinning, is precisely how writers think of story ideas and listen for the voice of poetry, introductions, or speeches. Suggest that he think about the five senses (what would the setting look like? sound like? smell like?), emotions, events, or family memories—or even look in his pockets. Given the space and time, an idea will begin to take form.

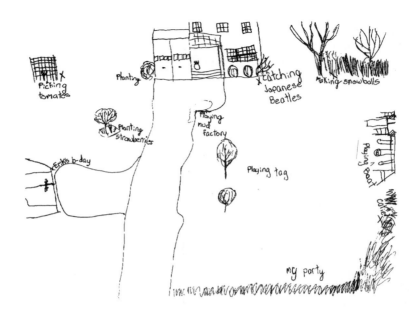

➤ Invite your child to draw a map of his favorite setting. Suggest that he write words to recall memories on different locations on the map. (See example above.) Then have him make an *x* on all of the places that a story happened. Ask, "Is there a story in this map that you would like to tell?"

➤ Cluster. Show your child how to cluster ideas for a writing assignment. Clustering is similar to webbing, except that words are permitted to flow freely and all ideas are accepted. Your child can begin with concrete words and move to more abstract ideas. Clustering will often bring out

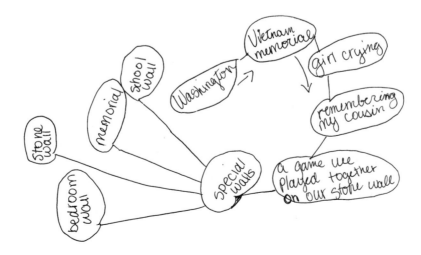

new relationships or ways of comparing information that were not recognized previously.

➤ Is your child really stuck? Have him try one of these suggestions:
- Write with your nondominant hand. What does this hand say about never getting the chance to write?
- Imagine that you're climbing a ladder and peeking in a window. What do you see?
- Imagine that you're in a room with six doors. Select one and open it. What's behind the door?
- Sketch before you begin writing. What comes to mind as you draw? Is there any part of the picture that you would like to write about?
- Study photographs in newspapers or magazines. What do they remind you of? Tell your own story.
- Read your favorite book to get into writing. Good books are the best models.

HAVE MORE TIME?

➤ Give your child hands-on experiences before writing about a nonfiction topic. Is your child writing about the solar system? Visit a planetarium. Is he writing about the gold rush? Pan for gold! Visit a museum, an aquarium, a nursery, or a local expert to help spark your child's imagination and give him a concrete experience to draw upon.

➤ Suggest that your child organize his thoughts visually through the use of a graphic organizer. He can use the 5W chart on page 201, or the Concentric Circle organizer on page 202 to make a chart like that on page 102, or he can create his own design.

Writing

Your child has an idea and has done a little bit of rehearsing: "I'm going to write a story about a house where green slime keeps coming out of the cracks and crevices." Now it's time to get down to the business of writing: "But I don't know how the people are going to find out about the inventor and his crazy idea of building houses without glue." Let your child know that it's okay not to have all the pieces in place before writing. Remind him of other times when he came up with a wonderful solution or changed his mind about the direction of a piece *as he was writing*. Suggest that he begin with what he has figured out so far, and assure him that he can stop and prewrite again if he gets stumped. A fifth grader might be inclined to put off writing until he has all the answers, which gives him a reason to procrastinate for a good long time. It's likely that

The 5 W's

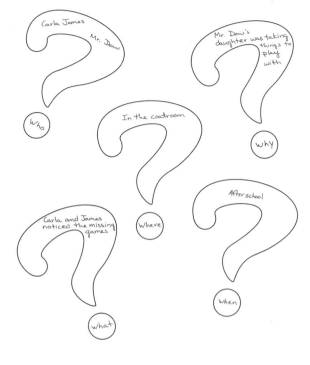

Who — Carla James, Mr. Dow

Why — Mr. Dow's daughter was taking things to play with

In the coatroom

Where

What — Carla and James noticed the missing games

When — After school

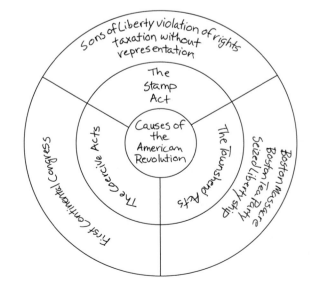

Causes of the American Revolution

The Stamp Act — Sons of Liberty violation of rights taxation without representation

The Coercive Acts — First Continental Congress

The Townshend Acts — Boston Massacre Boston Tea Party Seized Liberty ship

this child is still harboring a major misconception about writing—that is, that it must come streaming from the pencil to the paper perfectly, and on the first try. The best way to beat this misconception is to encourage your child to "get something down." Point out all that is working in this first draft so that your child can experience a sense of success with the writing stage and the confidence that any problems can be worked out later.

By fifth grade, most children are aware of several different writing forms—from the creative (fiction, poetry) to the practical (a friendly letter). Unlike the third grader who quickly writes the message of a thank-you note and then goes back to reshape the message into standard letter form, fifth graders are increasingly able to record their thoughts *and* concentrate on structure simultaneously. In other words, while writing about a story, the fifth grader thinks about having an exciting beginning and a satisfactory ending. While writing a report, he recalls the importance of a topic sentence, and the business letter is written with a consciousness of "the right way to do it," heretofore unseen.

This year, it is likely that your fifth grader will learn more about the following writing structures:

- fiction (quite possibly specific genres such as mysteries or science fiction)
- poetry
- personal narrative
- business letter
- report

Here are ways that you can help your child sharpen his skills using these forms.

Fiction

Perhaps your child has been writing stories since she was old enough to hold a pencil. Or, perhaps, this is the year she will discover her storytelling voice and the immense pleasure of creating whole worlds in which characters do as she beckons them to do—with sometimes hilarious, other times poignant, results.

In order to write good stories, one must understand what makes a good story. Somewhere during fifth grade, a child's analytical powers come into play. Now she can tell you whether or not a story has an exciting lead (the first few sentences) or whether the story's conflict was resolved successfully. She has begun to understand that good stories not only have a strong central character but that the character needs to solve the problem and, we hope, grow in the process. Little by little, she works what she is recognizing into her own writing.

TIPS FOR WRITING SUCCESS

You've helped your child prewrite, but she's still having trouble committing words to paper. Here are some additional suggestions to offer:

- As you write, pretend you are telling the information (story, poem) to your best friend.
- Try not to be a writer and an editor at the same time. If you don't know how to spell a word, write the word the way you think it is spelled and put "(sp?)" after it. You can look up the word later.

The best way to support a budding fiction writer is to: Read together and talk about why a story works or doesn't work well. (Caution: you don't want to turn your reading time into "quiz time." Share your knowledge and feelings about stories in the same way that you would share your love of baseball or music—in casual, spontaneous moments.) On the opposite page are some elements of fiction you might take a look at along with some books that lend themselves to talking about a specific element.

In addition to talking about fiction, try some of the following activities to help your child learn more about literary elements.

HAVE FIVE MINUTES?

➤ In a suspenseful story a character wants something badly, but everything and everyone seems to conspire against him. This "I want something but I can't get it" dilemma is what creates the tension. It's the very reason the reader keeps turning the pages. Point this conflict out to your child the next time you read a novel together. Then give your child a clearer understanding of story plot by playing No You Can't! State something you want. Have your child come up with as many "No you can't!" responses as she can. For example:

"I want to go to a movie tonight."
"No you can't! You can't find a sitter!"
"I want to go to a movie."
"No you can't! I've got a stomachache."
"I want to go to a movie."
"No you can't! The car's not working."
How many "No you can'ts" can your child come up with?

➤ Play What If? Take turns challenging one another with a difficult problem to resolve. For example: What if you were locked into the art museum at closing time? What would you do? (Read E. L. Konigsburg's *From the Mixed-Up Files of Mrs. Basil E. Frankweiler* to find out what one girl did when she ran away to the Metropolitan Museum of Art.) You might even want to use historical events such as: "What if dinosaurs had not become extinct?" "What if cars had not been invented?" "What if the British had won the Revolutionary War?" This exercise will help your child come up with creative resolutions in her own writing.

➤ Encourage your child to paint a picture or draw a map of her story setting. Tell her how the painting makes you feel or what you learned from the map. Later, have her show you how she developed the setting in her writing.

Characterization

What is the main character like? How do you know?
Are the characters believable? Why or why not?
Are you like the protagonist (main character)?
Is there an antagonist (bad guy) in this story?
How are you different from this character?
What other character does this character remind you of?
What skills does the character have that help him
   or her solve the problem?
Does the character change by the end of the story?

Books to Try

Ella Enchanted, by
Gail Carson Levine
(HarperCollins)
Wringer, by
Jerry Spinelli
(Knopf)

Setting

Can you imagine the setting? What helps you?
What mood does the setting put you in? Why?
Does the author use any words that help you see,
   hear, or smell the location?
Does the story take place in the past, present, or future?
How do you know when the story takes place?

*The Watsons Go to
Birmingham—1963,* by
Christopher Paul Curtis
(Bantam)
Lilly's Crossing, by Patricia
Reilly Giff (Delacorte)

Plot

What does the character really want?
What prevents the character from getting what
   s/he wants?
What is the main problem (conflict)
   in the story?
Was it easy to predict what would happen in the story?
   Why or why not?
Did you like the ending? Why or why not?
If you were the author, is there anything you would have
   done differently?

Frindle, by Andrew
Clements
(Simon & Schuster)
Sun and Spoon, by
Kevin Henkes
(Greenwillow)

Point of View

Who seems to be telling this story
   (narrator, main character)?
Do you like books written in first person
   (told by one character with the use of the word
   I as in "I thought I would like to take a swim")?

*The Ballad of Lucy
Whipple,* by Karen
Cushman (HarperCollins)
For Your Eyes Only,
by Joanne Rocklin
(Scholastic)

➤ Write "sudden poems" together. Take turns choosing a word—either a setting, such as *Laundromat,* or a person, such as *librarian.* Begin recording words that describe the place or person in a free verse poem. Here is how one group of children responded to the word *woods.*

Woods
By Raughley

Dark and spooky greenness
Make the woods
Dense and old
Make the woods
Whether quiet or noisy
Hot or cold
All of these
Make the woods

Woods
by Holly

It's quiet and shady in the woods
There is pitch, moss, pine trees, and leaves
Bits of sunlight shine
In between the branches
Birds sing and animals quietly
walk by.

➤ Play You Wouldn't Believe It! Although miracles are always welcome in real life, in stories solutions must make logical sense and result from the actions of the characters. If a story is about a child who is lost and has been struggling to survive in the woods for days, for instance, she cannot suddenly remember her magic powers and zap herself home. Stories that introduce simple solutions from nowhere—such as "Then he woke up and it was all a dream"—leave the reader feeling gypped or, worse, tricked. To help your child understand this concept, take turns thinking of stories you've read together and coming up with illogical conclusions. For instance: "Winnie the Pooh discovers that he is a real bear, not a stuffed bear, and he swims out of the flood." Or: "Aliens read the message in Charlotte's web and come and rescue Wilbur."

➤ Suggest that your fifth grader cut out pictures of people, places, and events from magazines and store them in a file. Whenever he needs help developing a setting, character, or plot, have him rummage through the file. He can work directly from one of the pictures or let the images remind him of a person or place in his own life. If your child is more inclined to do an activity *with* you than without you, cut out pictures for your own files. You might find pictures that spark ideas for house projects, gardening, and cooking, or simply pictures that make you feel good. Who knows, you might be inspired to write your own story or poem!

➤ Go to a movie together. Or rent one to see at home. Movie plots, settings, and characterizations are developed the same way, and follow the same rules, as those in literature. After the movie, discuss the characters (in what ways were they good? bad? both?), the believability of the setting, and whether or not the story problem was solved in a satisfactory way. Ask, "If you wrote this movie, is there anything you would have done differently?"

> If possible, give your child access to a computer. Computers free children from thinking about handwriting, spelling (there's always spell-check), and dreaded revisions since changes (moving text, adding and deleting text) are so easy to make. With a computer, fifth graders are far more likely to take creative risks—with astonishing results.

➤ Show; don't tell. When discussing how to create wonderful characters, professional writers repeat that creed over and over again. Give your child an example to help her understand the difference between telling about a character and showing the reader what the character is like.

Tell: John was a stubborn boy who often got his way.

Show: "I am not going to school," said John. He sat down on the bottom stair and would not move. His mother pleaded with him, she tried pulling him, she even tried bribing him with a week's worth of candy. John still would not move. "All right," his mother said finally. "You can stay home today."

Then write adjectives such as *kind, busy, brags a lot,* and *smart* on slips of paper. Take turns choosing a slip and writing about a character who demonstrates the quality. Have others guess the adjective chosen.

➤ Play the Mystery Character Game. Draw a container such as a trunk, a backpack, or a suitcase on a sheet of paper. Inside the container, write a list of things that might be in it really: a top hat, overalls, banana, bubble gum, four sheep, a tiara. Have your fifth grader, along with friends, invent characters who might own the odd assortment. For instance, the owner of this collection might be a female sheep farmer who moonlights as a magician, eats bananas for dinner, blows the biggest bubbles in Knox County, and is on her way to a coronation. See how many different characters they can come up with.

Poetry

Although it is likely that your child has been read poetry in school and that he's written a poem or two, most fifth graders are fairly limited in their understanding of poetry. There is a good reason for this. Poetry is a more abstract form of writing, and even at the beginning of fifth grade, children tend to be concrete rather than abstract thinkers.

When given the opportunity to write poetry, most fifth graders will attempt to write rhyming verse. Children are exposed to humorous rhyming verse more than any other form. What they don't realize, however, is that the rollicking, humorous verses of favorites Shel Silverstein (*Where the Sidewalk Ends*) and Jack Prelutsky (*A New Kid on the Block*) are extremely hard to write. Editors even discourage professional children's book writers from writing verse—it's simply too difficult to do well.

In addition to not knowing the rules of meter, fifth graders seldom have the vocabulary to write rhyming poems well. Their poetry is forced, and therefore it sounds trite. Does this mean, then, that fifth graders should be discouraged from writing rhyming poetry? Certainly not at home, where children should be encouraged to write to their own heart's desires. But by introducing your fifth grader to other forms of poetry, such as free verse, you will be giving him a whole new way of expressing himself. Children who discover free verse at the same time they are beginning to think about abstract concepts find a power in writing that can transform the way they think about themselves.

HAVE FIVE MINUTES?

➤ Look for poetry everywhere. Children become engaged in poetry through singing, chanting, rapping, and even dancing. Have your child make up new verses to favorite songs, raps, chants, jump rope jingles, or poems.

➤ Create poetry performances. Have your child choose background music to accompany the reading of a poem. Or have your child make up a modern dance to go with a piece of poetry.

➤ Write one-minute poems. Invite family and friends to sit around a table. Provide everyone with a few Post-it notes and a pencil. One person uses a watch with a second hand to time a minute, while everyone else writes a poem. Limiting the writing to one minute frees the writer to make quick associations. You will be amazed at the gems that come from an exercise like this.

➤ Write single-word poems. Invite your child to think of everything she can about a certain word. This brainstorming should be as wild and free ranging as possible. She can then write down these ideas—and more often than not, the list makes a leap to a poem.

➤ Encourage your child to collect words. He can cut the words from magazines or write them down on slips of paper when he sees or hears a word he likes. A word collection might contain words such as: *triple, transport, launch, dynamic, blueprint, song,* and *swing.* Have your child play with his collection from time to time, juxtaposing words in interesting combinations. Using some of the words above, one fifth grader wrote:

It launches into action
Doing its triple duty
Hearing the song
Making my feet move
Transporting me to where I want to.
It is the blueprint of me
My dynamic brain.

Listening to Poetry

Before asking your child to write poetry, give him plenty of opportunities to listen to and read poetry. Here are some collections for you to enjoy together:

- *Cool Salsa: Bilingual Poems on Growing Up Latino in the United States,* edited by Lori M. Carlson (Henry Holt)
- *Celebrating America: A Collection of Poems and Images of the American Spirit,* edited by Laura Whipple (Philomel)
- *The Dream Keeper and Other Poems,* by Langston Hughes (Knopf)
- *Extra Innings,* selected by Lee Bennett Hopkins (Harcourt Brace)
- *Grassroots,* by Carl Sandburg (Browndeer)
- *Harlem: A Poem,* by Walter Dean Myers (Scholastic)
- *If I Were in Charge of the World,* by Judith Viorst (Atheneum)
- *Laughing Out Loud, I Fly: Poems in English and Spanish,* by Juan Felipe Herrera (HarperCollins)
- *Mississippi Mud: Three Prairie Journals,* by Ann Warren Turner (HarperCollins)
- *Turtle in July,* by Marilyn Singer (Macmillan)

HAVE MORE TIME?

➤ Write similes (a comparison between two objects using *like* or *as*). Place an object, such as a button, on a table. Together, see how many similes you can write to describe the object. Encourage your fifth grader to go beyond the most obvious comparisons. Instead of "The button is as red as an apple," how about "The button is as red as a raspberry Popsicle"?

➤ Play the Simile Game. You will need a couple of markers or pens and a pile of index cards (or paper scraps). Make three piles of cards: one with nouns on the cards, one with verbs, and one with half similes such as "like a banana." Mix and match the cards, picking one from each pile, and read them to each other. Write down favorite similes. A poem might pop out of this exercise: "A Poem Roaring Like a Motorcycle."

➤ Listen to or read aloud ballads. A ballad is a poem that tells a story, often a sad one. Browse your local music store or library for folk ballads. Or look for picture books that are written as ballads, such as *The Ballad of the Pirate Queens*, by Jane Yolen (Harcourt Brace), or *Let Freedom Ring: A Ballad on Martin Luther King, Jr.*, by Myra Cohn Livingston (Holiday House).

➤ Suggest that your child make a book of her favorite poems—those of published authors as well as her own. Provide paper, poster board (cut slightly larger than the text paper), paints (for decorating the cover), and needle and dental floss (for sewing the book together). Or supply your poet with a blank book or notebook.

Near the cut-off to old Sante Fe
I met some boys chewing on hay
They thought it low class
But when trapped in Snow Pass
They rethought and called it gourmet.

I met, while driving my wagon,
A man, who said, "my hopes are saggin'
"my son thinks he's tough,
But when things get tough,
He's just weight that the oxen are
Draggin'."

by Willie
(grade 5)

➤Memorize and recite favorite poems. Choose one week in which each family member has a turn reciting a poem at the dinner table. (Even the youngest in your family can recite a line or two from a nursery rhyme.) You will not only be treated to lovely images or zany wordplay, your fifth grader will internalize the sound and structure of poetry—an essential skill for the writing of poetry.

Personal Narratives

Although your fifth grader doesn't know it, she has probably written more personal narratives, which are stories about oneself, than any other type of writing. Fifth grade is the year, however, when she focuses on a successful structure for a composition based on one of her real-life experiences. Here are some questions to help her:

- Think about your purpose. Do you want the narrative to entertain by being funny or suspenseful? Do you want to inform your audience? Do you want to persuade your audience to do or think something based on your own experience? Will your personal narrative have a message at the end?

- Write a captivating lead (opening paragraph) that will draw the reader into the story. You can do this by beginning with dialogue ("I will not climb that fence!") or a strong emotion (I have always hated painting). Some authors find it useful to begin a narrative right in the middle of the most exciting action ("I was standing at the top of the ledge in the middle of a hailstorm, with no apparent way to get down").

> ### LOOK FOR THIS BOOK
> One of the finest resources for teaching children to write poetry is *Poem-Making: Ways to Begin Writing Poetry*, by Myra Cohn Livingston (HarperCollins). In this book, she helps children begin with an image and make it come alive for readers.

- Include details that will help the reader experience what you experienced. Remember that you want to show the reader what the experience was like, rather than tell.

- Use dialogue. Dialogue can help the reader know what you were thinking and feeling.

- Write a conclusion. How did the experience change your life, or what have you come to believe now? If you are writing a humorous narrative, your conclusion should be funny, too.

HAVE FIVE MINUTES?

➤Help your child make a collage. Suggest she use a wide variety of materials: magazine photos, postcards, ticket stubs, package labels. Have her glue them together to make a visual description of herself. Is there one aspect of the collage or a memory revealed that she would like to write about?

➤ Suggest that your child look at photographs to help her recall details and the order of an event she wants to write about.

> While reading poetry together, point out these language techniques to help your child use imagery in his own fiction or poetry:
> **Alliteration:** Words that begin with the same sound, arranged in close proximity: Flies flitted furiously 'round my head. (Look for the picture book *Four Famished Foxes and Fosdyke,* by Pamela Duncan Edward, to help teach this concept.)
> **Metaphor:** A comparison of two different things to show a likeness between them. Unlike the simile, a metaphor does not use the words *like* or *as*: The day sprang from bed.
> **Onomatopoeia:** Words that sound like real sounds: *zoom, roar, ring*.

➤ Imagine a trunk. Help your child recall the details of a time or event by imagining a trunk in your attic or closet. Have her mentally open the trunk and tell you what it contains. For instance, if your child is writing about her first swimming lesson, she might recall the rubber bathing cap she was forced to wear, the yellow-flowered bathing suit with one strap that always fell down, the water wings her teacher slowly deflated, the Red Cross card or ribbon she received that told her she had passed the first level of instruction. If you actually have such a trunk in your attic, invite your fifth grader to rummage around inside it!

➤ Have your child call family members who could give her more details about her narrative topic.

HAVE MORE TIME?

➤ Encourage your child to keep a journal. By recording her thoughts and experiences on a regular basis, she will discover her own voice and be far more practiced at writing personal narratives. Most fifth graders love this form of writing and begin to identify themselves as "true writers" with the use of this form.

➤ Read from your own childhood journal! As you read excerpts, point out how parts could be shaped into a personal narrative. Tell your child which details you would include and why. And perhaps just as important, tell her which details you would delete and why.

Business Letters

Businesspeople are not the only ones who write business letters. Any time your fifth grader writes a letter requesting information or an autograph, a letter of complaint (or compliment) to a company, or a letter to the editor of a newspaper or magazine to express an opinion, he needs to use the business letter format. Here is the proper way to structure a business letter:

(heading) →	WendyWhistle PO Box 3349 Cumberland, ME 04021
(inside address) →	Washington Convention and Visitors Association 1212 New York Ave. NW Washington, DC 20005
(salutation followed by colon) →	Dear Sir or Madam:
(body) →	My family and I are going to visit Washington, DC, during the week of the fourth of July. We would like information on hotels and tours for children. I heard that the FBI tour is especially fun. Can you tell us how to get tickets? Thank you for taking the time to answer my questions.
(closing) →	Yours truly,
(signature) →	Wendy Whistle

HAVE FIVE MINUTES?

➤ Share your mail. We all receive business letters. Take a moment to select one from the pile that grabs your attention. Read it to your child. Point out the format, the purpose, and share your opinion of the letter with your fifth grader: "This one takes too long to get to the point" or "This one gives me all the information I need." Your child will be delighted to get a glimpse of your "official" mail.

➤ Read aloud a letter that you have written. Ask your child to give you feedback. Being asked to comment on a parent's writing is the ultimate compliment (and confidence builder) for a fifth grader.

➤ Suggest that your fifth grader write a letter in response to an article in a favorite magazine. Most children's magazines will publish letters from their readers.

➤ Planning a trip? Have your child write to the Chamber of Commerce to receive information and travel brochures about your destination.

➤If your child is writing a letter to express an opinion or a complaint, have him jot down a list of the points he wants to make and then decide what action he wishes the recipient of his letter to take. Thinking about these concretely will help him write a more effective letter.

HAVE MORE TIME?

Need an Address?

Finding an address for a company, pen pal, or celebrity might be easier than you think. Here are some sources.

For Companies:

• Look in your local phone book or business directory.

• Visit or call your local library and ask for the reference librarian, who will look up the number in sources such as the *Business Phone Book USA* (Darren L. Smith).

• Search the Internet.

For Published Authors:

• Send the letter to the publisher, whose address is listed on the copyright page of the book.

• Many authors also have web pages on the Internet and accept E-mail.

For Celebrities and Athletes:

• Use *The Kid's Address Book: Over 3,000 Addresses of Celebrities, Athletes, Entertainers and More . . .* , by Michael Levine.

➤Request an interview. If your child is writing a report, suggest he think of someone he could interview for more information. Then help him write a business letter to that person asking a couple of pertinent questions or requesting a face-to-face interview at another time.

Reports

Although writing a report might not be a new skill for your fifth grader, it's a skill she'll continue to develop through high school and beyond. To review, the steps of writing a report are:

1. Choose a topic.
2. Conduct research.
3. Organize your report.
4. Write and revise your report. Include the following parts:
   • introduction
   • body
   • conclusion

While writing a report, your fifth grader should be mindful of paragraph structure. Remind him that paragraphs are groups of sentences that combine the same idea. A good paragraph begins with a topic sentence and includes supporting details. The first line of each sentence should be indented.

Scientists have discovered dried-up river beds on mars! A spacecraft orbiting the planet took photos. The riverbeds are all different sizes. No one knows what happened to the water that once existed in these riverbeds.

topic sentence

details

When choosing a topic for a report, make sure your child selects one that he can handle. If the topic is too big, the material will overwhelm him. If the topic is too specialized, he won't be able to find enough information. For additional activities to help your child conduct research and organize the information for his report, see Study Skills, page 86.

HAVE FIVE MINUTES?

➤ Make a category chain. You or your fifth grader writes a topic, such as "animals" on a sheet of paper. Take turns drawing arrows from the front of the word or the back to record a broader topic or a subcategory (see example below). Keep going until neither of you can move in either direction. The last person to record a category wins. Before you begin a new game, discuss which categories would make good report topics and why.

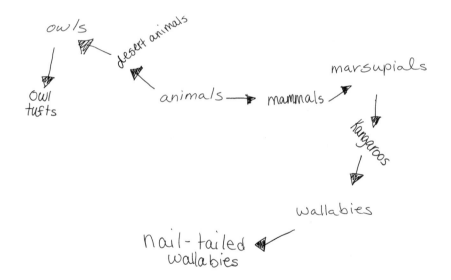

➤ Brainstorm a list of visual aids that would enrich the report. Your list might include a drawing, map, chart, or photographs. Remember to allow enough time for your child to draw graphics if needed.

HAVE MORE TIME?

➤ Help your child to go beyond encyclopedias to primary sources. If your child is writing a report on the Underground Railroad, for instance, help her find books that contain letters, diary excerpts, and personal accounts of the events and experiences. If possible, visit your local historical society for information. Your child might even be able to visit a home that has a secret passageway. Use the Internet to find out more about routes taken and important people who helped along the way. Look for poetry and spirituals that documented the trials or actually signaled the time to escape. You will not only teach your child important research skills, you will help make the topic come alive for her.

Revising

Good writing requires revising. It is the stage in which the author stands back and looks at her writing with an objective eye. It is the time to ask: "Is my meaning clear? Have I presented the information in the best order? Have I said all that I need to say? Or could I have said it with fewer words? Have I met my purpose and will I reach my audience?"

Many people think that revising is editing. That is, that revision is the time to make sure all the *i*'s are dotted, the *t*'s are crossed, and the spelling is correct. But revising and editing are very different processes. During the revision stage, a writer makes changes in the *content*, not the mechanics, of a piece of writing.

Many fifth graders say, "I hate to revise." And many a fifth grade teacher has been heard to say, "Fifth graders aren't ready to revise." But the truth is that most writers, even professionals, resist revision. We all wish that we could reach the end of a sentence, slap the pencil down, and exclaim "Done" and have it be so. To communicate effectively, however, writers must take some time to put themselves in the place of the reader. And the more a writer works on revision, the more he comes to value this stage.

Two things are extremely useful in helping the fifth grader to revise. One is to offer to "confer" with your child. It is hoped that your fifth grader is participating in writing conferences at school where the teacher or other students listen to her read her writing aloud and then respond by telling her which parts were clear, which parts informed or entertained, and which parts, perhaps, were still hard to understand. If so, your child can show you how to conference at home. If not, here are a few guidelines for offering to be your child's audience:

- After listening to your child's writing, comment on what is working well. Be very specific. Responding with "That's wonderful" is not helpful because your child cannot determine precisely what made the piece wonderful and therefore she cannot repeat the success. If you say, however, "You used so many words that involved my senses, I felt like I was standing in the orchard with you," your child will know that she was effective in creating imagery.

- Ask questions to indicate places that might need more work: Saying "Where did the tractor in the orchard come from?" is far more helpful than saying "This part is confusing."

The other way that parents and teachers can help fifth graders revise is to suggest specific, rather than general, assignments. Telling a fifth grader "You've written a first draft, now it's time to revise" is far too general and overwhelming. Suggesting, however, that your child take a moment to consider the title—Does it indicate what the piece is about? Is it a grabber? Will it make readers want to read the piece?—helps the child go back to his writing for an important second look.

As your child becomes more practiced in revising, she may read her text out loud, suddenly see a place where she left out words or did not make her meaning clear, and then run off to make corrections. Rejoice. Your child has begun to realize that revision is part of her job as a writer.

HAVE FIVE MINUTES?

➤ Go ahead and verbally revise the literature that you read aloud together. Don't be afraid to say, "I would have used the word *mashed* instead of *folded*." Or "This beginning is dull. I would have begun the story when Carol was climbing the fence." Get your child to join in on the act. Ask, "Did you like that ending? How would you have ended this book instead?" Before long, your child will demonstrate the knowledge that stories can (and should be) improved upon.

➤ Ask the simple question "What is your story (essay, article) about?" If she has a hard time answering the question, she might require a little help in focusing her thoughts and/or organizing her writing.

DID YOU SEE THIS REPORT?

If your child wishes to write a report that stands out from all of the others, have him try one of these techniques:

- Write the report from the point of view of a newspaper reporter. For instance, he could pretend that he is a reporter interviewing Paul Revere to get facts about the American Revolution.
- Use fictional techniques such as setting a scene or telling a story. He could use actual quotes to make people seem more real and build suspense.
- Write an intriguing title and a dramatic opening.
- Read a novel that relates to your subject. This will help the material seem more meaningful and will help your child write with more understanding and interest.

➤ Have your child brainstorm a list of opening lines or endings for her piece and then choose the one she likes best. This will help develop the concept that writers explore different ideas before making a choice.

➤ Self-interview. The next time your fifth grader comes running to tell you she's done, have her stop and ask herself a series of questions about her writing. Here are questions she might use:
  • Does my story (article, learning log, letter) make sense?
  • Have I given the reader enough information?
  • Have I written more information than the reader needs?
  • Do I have an exciting beginning?
  • Do I end in a satisfying place?

➤ Offer to read her written work aloud. Often a writer can catch places to revise when she actually *hears* her work for the first time.

HAVE MORE TIME?

➤ Have your child choose a paragraph from a story she's written. Show her how to change the verb tense from past to present (or vice versa). For example, the sentence "I walked into the shed and saw an old blanket resting on the floor" would become "I walk into the shed and see an old blanket resting on the floor." How does a change in verb tense change the writing? Your fifth grader might suddenly become so intrigued with the immediacy of the story in first person that she rewrites her story or begins another.

➤ Musical revision. Even if your child doesn't sing in a chorus or play an instrument, she has probably listened to enough music to know that in musical scores there are fast passages, slow ones, loud ones, and soft ones. Suggest she use different-color markers to underline the fast moving action and the slower moving descriptions in her own writing. Is there a variety? Does she want or need more of one or the other?

➤ Show your child how to revise her writing with the use of a computer. Children are much more apt to add or delete text, or move text around, when they know that their changes won't require hours of copying work over by hand. They can try revisions in the word processing program, and if they don't like them, they can return the text to its original state. They can even keep several drafts of the same story for comparison. If you don't have access to a computer, see if your child's school or the local library provides computers for public use.

➤ If you don't have access to a computer, show your child how to use these revision techniques:
- carêts (^), for inserting text above a line.
- arrows (>), for showing where text should be moved.
- asterisks (*), for marking where a large block of text should be added.
- spiderlegs, what teachers call slips of paper with additions on them that are taped to pages.
- lines (——) through words for deletions.

Editing

How do children best learn the skills of spelling, punctuation, and language usage? Through reading and writing, writing and reading. While writing a story, for example, the fifth grader wonders how to differentiate between two characters who are speaking. He knows about quotation marks, but his story is confusing. Later, he picks up the story of Johnny Tremain and notices, perhaps for the first time, that each time a new character speaks the author begins a new paragraph. Not only that, but the fifth grader is reminded to use explanatory phrases such as "he said." He looks carefully to see how the author punctuates the phrases and makes a mental note to use commas in his own writing.

Wouldn't it be easier to just come right out and teach these skills? Not necessarily. When skills are taught in isolation—that is, when they are introduced through worksheets and workbooks—they have no immediate relevance to the child. They are simply an exercise to get through on the way to doing better, more meaningful activities. They are seldom remembered when writing time comes, partly because the fifth grader had no use for them when they were introduced.

On the other hand, children who read and write often know that both what they say (content) and how they say it (convention) matter to a reader. In order for the reader to appreciate the message, the writing must appear without distracting errors. After your child has successfully completed the writing and revision process, he is ready and usually quite willing to edit. After all, he hopes to receive a successful grade, positive feedback, or even acceptance for publication of his work. At this stage—the editing stage—the child has both reason and motivation to learn standard practices.

Suggest that your child act as his own editor first. After he has completed his last revision, give him a colored pencil (just like the editors in publishing houses use) and suggest that he go through and make any changes he deems necessary. He might make sure that he has used capital letters and punctuation appropriately, and he might circle words he suspects are misspelled. (Good spellers know when a word doesn't look right and that they must self-correct.) Have him look up the correct spellings in the dictionary or in a Spellex Speller (these can be purchased at bookstores).

After he has edited his work, offer to take a look at his writing. Do not expect perfection. He is a growing writer and will benefit more from acceptance of his work than from a long list of things to fix. In fact, one of the best exercises for both of you is for you to take a moment and tell him everything that you notice he's doing *right*. Next, inform him of one or two rules that he could follow in his writing. Providing more than one or two at a time is counterproductive. After two lessons, he's likely to resist listening, knowing that there isn't any way that he's going to remember "all that."

If you wish, have him record the new rules you introduced on an Editor's Checklist form, page 203. The next time he edits his own work, he can check to make sure he has incorporated what you taught him last. If your child's teacher has provided a list of criteria for acceptable writing, add these items to the checklist. (When one list is full, toss it out and start another. Do not include skills that are used fairly regularly—knowing, of course, that we all leave out a comma now and then!)

HAVE FIVE MINUTES?

➤ Punctuation translation. Next time you're reading together, explain that the purpose of punctuation is to help the reader understand what to do with his or her voice. If the reader can't stop or pause now and then, the words jumble together and the meaning is lost. Have your child read a passage aloud and say "Stop" when she comes to a period, "Pause" when she comes to a comma, and "Wow!" when she comes to an exclamation point. When she's got those words down, have her say "Listen" when she comes to quotation marks and "It's coming up" when she sees a colon. You might even hear her muttering these words as she writes and directs her own audience.

➤ Give your child a sheet of twenty words and challenge her to find the ten that are misspelled. Children rarely get the opportunity to realize that they know more about spelling than they think they do.

Your fifth grader might be ready to question and edit the following conventions in his writing:

- Are any of the paragraphs too long (too many ideas combined)?
- Do you divide words correctly (between syllables, one-syllable words are never divided)?
- Have you used a consistent verb tense (either the past or the present)?
- Have you used apostrophes when something belongs to someone?
- Have you used commas in series, dates, and when the reader needs to pause?
- Do you use quotation marks around dialogue?
- Do you begin a new paragraph each time someone new speaks?
- Have you included "s/he said" when needed?

➤ Recording dialogue. Should one spy on others in public places? Professional writers do it all the time! It's a great way to collect realistic dialogue. Suggest that your child bring her notebook the next time she's spending time at a doughnut shop or hamburger palace. She can record snippets of real-life conversations that could very well lead to a new story. Remind her to use quotation marks around the dialogue to separate it from her other spy notes.

➤ Settle arguments. Having a sibling dispute? Does your fifth grader think that something's not fair? Write down the problem. Give each child an opportunity to speak and record his or her thoughts in quotation marks with explanatory phrases: "I never get to watch the show I want," Danielle said. Then ask for suggestions on ways to solve the problem. You will not only be modeling the way to write dialogue, you will help your child feel as if you take her problems seriously.

HAVE MORE TIME?

➤ Play the Wordy Wordsmith Game. An overuse of adjectives and adverbs leads to wordy writing. Take turns writing and sharing verbose phrases. Challenge one another to replace the adjectives or adverbs with precise words. Here are some examples: The strong, lashing rain beat down on me. (Rain pelted me.) The singer with the exalted voice seemed quite sure of herself as she slowly sang the high note. (The soprano held high C with confidence.)

If your child struggles with spelling, she might have a spelling disability. Discuss this possibility with your child's teacher and then help your child to become comfortable using a variety of resources to assist with spelling, such as electronic and computer spell-checkers and other people who are good at spelling and can provide a word now and then.

Reading and Writing Enrichment

Perhaps your child breezed through the assessment provided with this book and is ready for new challenges. Or perhaps your child absolutely loves to read and write and you are looking for new ways to stimulate his thinking. Maybe your child has strong critical thinking skills and is ready to look at writing or reading from yet another perspective. Or perhaps you homeschool your child and are looking for the right activity to spark your own—as well as your child's—imagination. If so, this chapter has been included for you.

Please note that some of the activities require a more sophisticated form of abstract thinking. Until the end of fifth grade, many children remain quite concrete and literal in their thinking. One of the greatest pleasures for a parent of a ten-year-old is watching a child's mind open to new possibilities in thought.

In recent decades, educators have increasingly used practices of "metacognition" in their teaching. This means that they not only present students with a body of knowledge, they help children learn *how* to learn. They do this by discussing learning strategies, by giving children meaningful learning experiences to motivate them and relate learning to, and by modeling their own thinking. In other words, they help children think by "thinking out loud." This is a teaching technique that parents are particularly effective at using at home. Do some of the activities suggested here, and take your child through your own thinking process: "Before I began reading this book on lawmaking, I tried to think of everything I know about the American government. But I realized that I still get the branches of government confused. I'm going to begin reading, but if the author doesn't tell me what I need to know or if the information doesn't make sense, I think I'll look up government in the encyclopedia, learn some facts, and then try reading this book again." Sharing how you learn while you learn together is a wonderful gift to give your child.

HAVE FIVE MINUTES?

➤ Have your child design a travel brochure for an extremely unpleasant place. Your child might enjoy writing "tongue in cheek" as she promotes vacation spots such as the middle of an iceberg or the center of the earth.

➤ Collect proverbs. As you know, proverbs are short, pithy statements, often metaphors, that gently advise. "Don't count your chickens before they hatch" is a proverb. Categorize them according to their source (the Bible, fables, etc.). Or look for patterns in the way in which they are written: two words ("Time flies"); alternatives ("Sink or swim"); or rhyming proverbs ("An apple a day keeps the doctor away"). Look for proverbs that recommend opposite actions, such as "Look before you leap" and "He who hesitates is lost." Suggest that your child illustrate proverbs either figuratively or literally. Try writing proverbs of your own.

Books for the Gifted Reader

Fifth grade is the year that many children begin sneaking into the adult shelves of libraries. (Stephen King's books have strong appeal for middle graders—whether we approve of them or not.) Or they discover a wonderful category of children's literature known as "young adult books." But even the young adult category is divided—those for younger sophisticated readers and those for children ready to handle more mature topics. Most fifth graders fall into the former category. Ask your children's librarian to point out books that have sophistication—but content appropriate for your child. You might want to bring home one of these books if you haven't already:

• *A Wrinkle in Time,* by Madeline L'Engle (Farrar Straus Giroux)
• *The Sign of the Beaver,* by Jean Craighead George (Houghton Mifflin)
• *Out of the Dust,* by Karen Hesse (Puffin)
• *The Hobbit,* and others, by J. R. R. Tolkien (Houghton Mifflin)
• *The Moorchild,* by Eloise McGraw (McElderry)
• *The View from Saturday,* by E. L. Konigsburg (Aladdin)

➤ Suggest that your child make a list of words that he hates the sound of. You might help him by sharing a few of your own: *disease, fat, dear*. You might find that once he gets going the list goes on for days. Often a list like this will spark a poem, a cartoon, or a letter to the editor. When he's grown tired of this list, suggest that he write a list of words that he loves the sound of.

Words I don't like the sound of

Leaches
Puss
Garbage
ants
weeds
crash
fat
brush
vacuum
yogurt

➤ Play Twenty Questions based on books and characters from books.

HAVE MORE TIME?

➤ Myth making. Every culture has stories to explain creation or natural phenomena. Compare myths from two different cultures. How are they the same? How are they different? Encourage your child to write his own myth describing how one aspect of life came to be.

➤ Encourage your child to become a scribe at a local nursing home. People often need help with letter writing. Sometimes they want their family stories written down or captions placed on the backs of photographs. Go along with your child to help him get started. Before long, he will know the rewards of helping in this way.

➤ Try image making. Begin by making a fairly large collection of "splatter paintings." You and your fifth grader can do this by splattering different colors of paint on a sheet of paper with a toothbrush or by blowing drops of paint across the paper with a straw (watercolor paint works well).

When the papers are dry, look for shapes and images in the papers: "This looks like a woman swimming" or "This looks like a dog jumping in the air." Use some of the pages with images to cut from. Choose other papers to be background pages. As you cut out images and glue them on the background sheets, a story might begin to emerge. You and your child can continue cutting and pasting to bring the whole story into realization. Write text directly on the pages or mount the pages on separate sheets and bind them into a book.

➤Visit art museums. Encourage your child to read the captions about the paintings. If you read a long piece about an artist's life, share the highlights with your child. Send your child on a scavenger hunt. Have her search for images that can be found in the museum; an ugly dog or a grumpy man in a sunken ship can provide fun, motivation, and hooks for your child to remember what she sees.

➤Have your child write a script for a play or "television show." Suggest that she decide what she'd like the story to be about (she might want to use a story map such as the one on page 204 to prewrite) and divide the story into acts (acts are like chapters in a book). Remind her that with a play, the story is told entirely through action and dialogue. Show her how to indicate who speaks in a script and to record stage directions. Encourage her to perform her play; record it on videotape if you can. (If your child writes a script for a pretend television show, she might want to script some commercials, too!)

PUBLISH OR PERISH

There are several exceptional magazines for children written by children. Encourage your child to submit a story, cartoon, riddle, joke, or drawing to one of the following (you might want to write ahead to request a sample copy and the magazine's writer's guidelines:

Stone Soup
Box 83
Santa Cruz, CA 95063

Shoe Tree
215 Valle del sol Drive
Santa Fe, NM 87501

Wombat, Inc.
Box 8088
Athens, GA 30603

Word Dance
Playful Productions
P.O. Box 10804
Wilmington, DE 19850-0804

Young Voices
P.O. Box 2321
Olympia, WA 98507

Math Exercises

Problem Solving

"Mom, can you help me with my math?"

"Sure, honey," you say. Then you glance at the problem: "A plane left New York City at 1:00 P.M. It landed in Chicago 1½ hours later. Then it flew for 3½ more hours and landed in Los Angeles. If it reached Los Angeles at 3:30 P.M., how long was it on the ground in Chicago?"

You feel a familiar sinking in the pit of your stomach. Your eyes begin to glaze over. You tell yourself, "This is fifth grade math. I can do this. After all, I *was* in fifth grade myself once upon a time. . . ." Meanwhile, your mind shouts, "Too many numbers!"

Somewhere around the time that their children enter fifth grade, most parents—even those who regularly use higher level mathematics in their own work—begin to question their own ability to help their children with math. For some, it's a case of math anxiety: "I have always hated math." For others, it's a matter of time: "These problems are so much more complicated. It's not just a quick fix anymore." For still others, it's the numbers themselves: "I never *did* understand fractions."

At the same time, parents know instinctively, if not from experience, that a fear of math—or even a lack of confidence—can be debilitating. Much of the math that you use in the course of your daily life is, in fact, fifth grade math.

What do those statistics from your insurance agent actually mean? How do you figure out a 15 percent tip? Should you take the job with the better salary or the better health plan? How many boxes are you going to need to pack the books on that bookshelf? In short, your child's command of fifth grade skills and his confidence in his ability to use those skills will affect not only his future success in mathematics but his ability to cope in the world.

Luckily, even if your own understanding of fractions, decimals, and probability is pretty shaky, there is still much you can do to give your child the confidence he needs to move forward in math. How? By creating an environment that builds your child's confidence as a problem solver. Remember, *all* of mathematics is problem solving. Therefore, every time you encourage your child to solve his own problems ("I don't know, how *are* you going to do both Children's Theater and Little League this year?"), cheer his successes ("Boy, how did you figure *that* one out?"), and downplay his mistakes ("Oh, well, it was worth a try"), you are strengthening your child's problem-solving abilities and giving him the skills he needs to be a confident mathematician. The equation is simple: The more practice in problem solving your child has, the better he will be in math. Here are three things you can do to help:

1. Be happy. (Mathematics *can* be fun.)
2. Don't worry. (Model persistence and optimism.)
3. Be flexible. (Share problem-solving strategies.)

Having Fun with Mathematics

HAVE FIVE MINUTES?

➤ Follow your child's passion. What's the current rage? Football? Beading? Egyptian hieroglyphics? Watch for opportunities to gently incorporate math into your child's beloved pastime. Play with sports statistics. Explore Native American beading patterns. Make up a set of hieroglyphics for your own family.

➤ Ask math riddles. Math riddles are great time-passers in the car. Toss out a riddle like one of those listed below, then see if your child can make up a few of his own. Books of brainteasers are available in your library or bookstore. Here are a few to get you started:

A QUESTION OF TIME

Much of the frustration parents feel about helping their children with math in the upper grades has to do with time. Many parents find that the problems their fifth graders bring home simply take more figuring out than they did a year ago. The frustration of trying to figure out a complex math problem and fix dinner at the same time is not only ineffectual, it can actually destroy any positive feelings your child has about math. Try setting aside a quiet time just for math—the same kind of time you might already have established for reading together. You might choose to extend your fifth grader's bedtime by a half hour so you can give him your undivided attention after younger children are asleep, or you might suggest waking him early for a math session with your first cup of coffee. Structuring a special time will tell your child that both he and math are important to you.

- Mom is five times older than my sister. Sis is thirty years younger than Dad. Dad is four times my age. If Sis is seven, how old am I? [10]

- Continue this pattern: A, 100, Z, 1, B, 99, Y, 2 . . . [C, 98, X, 3, D, 97, W, 4, E, 96 . . .]

- What's wrong with this picture? A family of five ordered a pizza. Each member of the family ate ⅔ of the twelve-slice pizza. [If five people ate ⅔ of a pizza each, they would have eaten 3⅓ pizzas.]

- I want to plant ten flower plants in five rows of four plants each. Can I do it? [Yes. Plant the flowers in the shape of a star.]

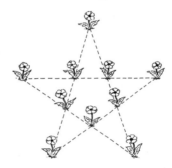

➤ Wow your child with the wizardry of math. A couple of tricks up your sleeve will go a long way toward helping your child see the wonder of numbers and might even earn you some much deserved respect as a mathematician. Here are a couple of good examples of the wizardry of nine.

Wizard One
1. Choose a number (any number).   637
2. Subtract the sum of the numbers' digits.   637 – 16 = 621
3. The answer will be divisible by 9.   621 ÷ 9 = 69
   BUT WAIT! THERE'S MORE!
4. Add together the digits of the answer. Keep adding until you get one digit. Guess what! That digit is 9!   6 + 2 + 1 = 9

Wizard Two
1. Choose a number with more than one digit.   364
2. Rearrange the digits to make another number.   643
3. Subtract the smaller number from the larger number.   643 – 364 = 279   279 ÷ 9 = 31
4. The answer is divisible by 9!
5. And, yep, you guessed it. Add those digits together until you get one digit. Nine again!   2 + 7 + 9 = 18   1 + 8 = 9

Wizard Three

1. Divide any number by 9.
2. Add the digits of the dividend (the number you're dividing into) until you come up with one digit.
3. The number you come up with is the remainder!
4. Here's the catch: If the sum of the digits is 9, there *is* no remainder.

$152 \div 9 =$

$1 + 5 + 2 = 8$

$152 \div 9 = 16 \, R8$

➤ Play with alternate solutions.

"How are we going to get this room cleaned before the Ladies' Aid Society arrives?"
"A bulldozer?"
"That's one idea. Any others?"

HAVE MORE TIME?

➤ Play games. In many ways, fifth grade is the prime of childhood. Your child has the skill, self-discipline, and experience to enjoy games as he has never enjoyed them before. A good game of chess or Monopoly or Risk will stretch your fifth grader (and you!) in new directions without either one of you even noticing it. But don't overlook a simple game of sandlot baseball or tag as well. Every time your child decides whether to go for the double or when to run for home base, he is using problem-solving skills.

➤ Take advantage of your fifth grader's love of trivia. This is the year you will find your fifth grader poring over the *Guinness Book of World Records* or *The Book of Lists*. Take that fascination a step further by posing "I Wonders":

• It says here that the person with the biggest feet currently known wears a size 26 shoe. I wonder how long his feet measure in inches.
• The fastest luge speed is 85.38 miles per hour. I wonder how many feet per second that is.
• If Pablo Picasso produced 578,000 pieces of artwork in his lifetime and he lived 78 years, does that mean he produced at least one piece of art every day he was alive?

> ### GAMES FOR MATH
> The following games are particularly good for reinforcing number sense and problem-solving skills. For additional suggestions, check *Kids' Games*, by Phil Whistle, and *Games of the World*, by Frederick Greenfield.
> Backgammon
> Battleship
> Card games of any sort
> Chess
> Cribbage
> Darts
> Go
> Maniacal
> Other
> Parcheesi
> Quarto
> Yoke

➤ Read mysteries together. There's nothing like a good whodunit to stretch those problem-solving muscles and strengthen the powers of deductive reasoning.

➤ If your family is planning a trip, ask your fifth grader to help you figure out the arrangements:

- What is the best way to reach our destination?
- How much will the trip cost?
- How many miles do we have to go?
- How long will it take to get there?
- What other arrangements do we have to make?

Great Deduction, Fifth Grader

Mysteries for middle graders range from Encyclopedia Brown to Sherlock Holmes himself. Here are a few of the best.

- *House with a Clock in Its Walls,* by John Belarus (Dial)
- *The Master Puppeteer,* by Katherine Paterson (Avon)
- *Mystery on Bleaker Street,* by William Hooks (Knopf)
- *The Spook Birds,* by Eve Bunting (Whitman)
- *The Westing Game,* by Ellen Raskin (Dutton)

➤ Ask, "If we decided to paint your room, what would we need to consider?" Remind your child to consider aesthetics as well as numbers. What happens if he loses his taste for black-and-white stripes within the next year?

➤ Explore the math behind simple toys. Albert Einstein once said that his lifelong fascination with mathematics and the laws of nature could be traced back to a compass his father gave him when he was five. Give your child the opportunity to use and explore simple devices such as a kaleidoscope or a pendulum and see how much fun improving one's skills of observation and hypothesis can be.

Most of the following devices are inexpensive and can be easily obtained at hardware stores or educational toy stores.

balance scale	kaleidoscope	photo-sensitive paper
barometer	kite	prism
binoculars	light meter	Slinky
compass	magnets	thermometer
electrical circuit	magnifying glass	tuning fork
gyroscope	pendulum	

Modeling Persistence in Problem Solving

Watch your fifth grader trying to perfect a free throw or a cartwheel. Throw after throw, cartwheel after cartwheel—no matter how many missed baskets or hard landings, your child keeps at it with a grim determination worthy of

Alexander the Great. And eventually, she does begin to hit a few baskets or land neatly on her feet.

Now watch that same child attempt to complete a sheet of math homework. She scribbles down an answer, gazes off into space, wraps her pencil in her hair, then decides the pencil needs sharpening, gets a drink of water, sits back down, scans the next problem, begins to doodle. Finally, she throws down her pencil in frustration and announces, "I just don't *get* this!"

It comes as no surprise to most parents that their children don't show the same level of commitment and determination in math that they do in basketball or gymnastics. A fifth grader will tell you simply, "Well, I *like* basketball, and I don't *like* math." Yet, according to some mathematicians, it is that very quality of persistence that leads to eventual success in math—which, in turn, leads to liking math (which leads to greater patience and persistence, which leads to additional success, which leads to liking math even more . . .).

Fostering a persevering attitude, however, takes more than the occasional admonishment to "try, try again." Like any inner drive, persistence is nurtured through experience. So, how do you go about giving your child persistence-friendly experiences? It might help to remember a few guidelines:

BLAME THE PROBLEM

Many children—and adults—assume that if they can't solve a problem immediately, it's their own darned fault. They haven't studied hard enough, or they don't know the right math, or they weren't born with that all-important "good at math" gene. Whenever your child comes up against a sticky problem (in life as well as in schoolwork), say, "Wow, this one is a real killer!" or "How are we going to figure this one out?" Placing the blame squarely on the problem tells your child that you recognize its difficulty without reinforcing negative thoughts she might already have about her math abilities or giving her an excuse for not even giving it a go.

1. Lighten up. Your child knows that the fate of the world does not rest upon how many pieces of pizza Jack or Jill ate. Part of what deadens math is a pervading attitude of excruciating seriousness. Inject some humor wherever you can. It will do wonders.

2. Encourage guessing. Guessing, or estimating, is an important problem-solving strategy (see the list of problem-solving strategies on page 135). Although guessing is usually a slow process, it is a vital part of logical thinking. If you encourage guessing, little by little your child will come to understand that certain bits of information make guessing easier. Having the patience and understanding to ask the right questions is an important skill in life as well as in math.

3. Respect wrong answers. Try your best to dispel the myth that people who are good at math always get the right answer. The best mathematicians usually go through a lot of wrong answers before they get to the right one.

More often than not, wrong answers represent a lot of hard work. Think of wrong answers not as "wrong" but as "partially right." Look for what is right and move ahead from there.

4. Assume that good problem solving takes time. Somewhere along the line, many children (and adults) get the impression that people who are good at math just "get it." Your child knows that it takes time to read a book. The good thinking that goes into wrestling with a problem also takes time. Starting with that assumption can defuse a lot of the frustration of problem solving.

HAVE FIVE MINUTES?

➤ Find and use the problem-solving opportunities in your child's daily life. Drawing pictures, playing sports, cooking meals, building models—practically every activity your child does is steeped in some sort of mathematics. Gently point out the mathematics in the situation. Then let your child's own interests and determination do the rest.

➤ Ask questions and then listen carefully. When your child comes up with a solution to a problem, either in math or in daily life, ask, "How did you get that?" Most teachers don't have time to figure out how each of the twenty-five children in a class is thinking about a problem. You do. The question "How did you get that?" offers you a window into your child's thinking process. Be sure to ask the question about correct answers as well as incorrect answers. Otherwise, your child might assume that "How did you get that?" is merely a euphemism for "That's wrong."

➤ Phrase family dilemmas as problems to be solved. Talk about "The Case of the Missing Trombone Music" or "The C Files: Unexplained Disappearances at 321 Cedar Avenue." When you find that your child's first softball game is at exactly the same time as her brother's first piano recital, ask, "Okay, how are we going to solve this problem?" and then model tenacity and flexibility in coming up with a solution.

HAVE MORE TIME?

➤ Encourage individual hobbies. By fifth grade, many children's daily lives have become a series of structured activities: school, Scouts, sports, lessons, birthday parties, and special events. Persistence takes the form of outside demands: Do this and you will get your Scouting badge; do that or you won't make the track team. An individual hobby—drawing or stamp collecting or making electronic gadgetry, for example—requires a different kind of motivation, an inner drive and persistence.

➤ Pose a problem you don't know how to solve. Post it on the refrigerator or the family bulletin board. Then watch the entire family model persistence and determination. Here are a couple of easy ones to get you started:

- Can you hold one end of a piece of rope in each hand and tie a knot in the middle without letting go of either end? [Yes. Tie your arms in a knot.]
- In a dish of red, yellow, and purple jelly beans, all but four are red, all but four are yellow, and all but four are purple. How many jelly beans are in the dish? [six]
- How can you drop an uncooked egg four feet onto a concrete floor without breaking it? (Drop it from five feet above the floor. It won't break for four feet.)

After your family has had some practice solving brainteasers, suggest that you start making up your own. You'll be surprised how easy it is once you've learned a format or two.

➤ Give the answer to a problem—for example, "1,000 cows." Then see how many problems you and your child can come up with that can be solved with that answer.

➤ Play Pico, Fermi, Bagels. Like the commercial game Mastermind, this game requires patience and persistence. You can make it as difficult as you wish simply by adding more digits. Here are the rules:

Family Teasers
You can find books of brainteasers and puzzles in your local library or bookstore. You might also want to keep an eye out for *Zigzag*, a children's magazine full of brainteasers put out by the publishers of *Games* magazine.

- *The Adventures of Penrose the Mathematical Cat* and *Penrose Presents My Best Math Puzzles,* by Theoni Pappas (Wide World Publishing)
- *Brain Teasers* or any book in the Mind Benders series, (World Book)
- *Mathamusements,* by Raymond Blum (Sterling)
- *Think-a-Grams,* by Evelyne M. Graham (Critical Thinking Press)
- *Super Math Tricks,* by Zondraw Knapp (Lowell House)

PICO, FERMI, BAGELS

1. One player chooses a secret number and tells the others the number of digits in the number.
2. The second player tries to guess the number.
3. The first player responds to each guess by giving the following clues:
   PICO: *One* of the digits is correct, but it is in the *wrong* place.
   FERMI: *One* of the digits is correct and in the *right* place.
   BAGELS: *None* of the digits is correct.
4. The second player keeps a record of guesses and responses.
5. Believe it or not, eventually the second player will guess the number!

➤ Teach your child the cardinal rule of brainstorming: *There are no bad ideas.* Fifth graders like resolution and can be quick to criticize ideas and solutions that don't appear to make sense. Encourage your child to come up with as many ideas as possible by jotting ideas down in a web and seeing how many different circles he can come up with before settling on one solution.

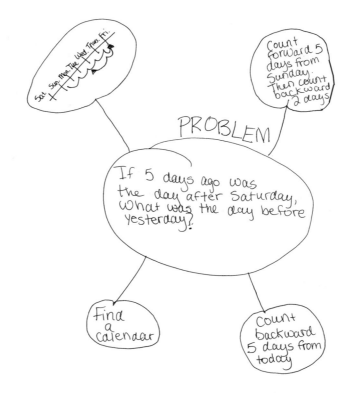

Sharing Problem-Solving Strategies

Word problems. If the mere mention of those two words brings thoughts of tears and frustration, you are not alone. Most likely, you have your own memories of trying to decode "If train A leaves the station at 6:45 and train B leaves at 10:30 . . ." Or perhaps you have already experienced a wrestling session with your child over how to approach a sheet of homework.

Don't give up just yet. Problem solving, like any skill, takes practice and know-how. Many children (and adults) don't realize that there is more than one way to solve any given problem. Share with your child a few of the different problem-solving strategies listed below. You might be surprised at how much more often you begin to hear, "Oh, yeah! *Now* I get it!"

1. Use objects.
2. Draw a picture or make a model.
3. Make a chart.
4. Guess and check.
5. Look for a pattern.
6. Work backward.
7. Make a table or an organized list.
8. Do a simpler or similar problem.

HAVE FIVE MINUTES?

➤Whenever you encounter a problem in your everyday life, ask, "What do we need to know to solve this problem?" Say, "Okay, you and your sister both need rides to your games on Wednesday night. Now, what do we need to know to solve this problem?"

➤Talk about the language of word problems. In word problems, very often the words themselves get in the way. A child who knows the mathematical expression 3 + 2 might not necessarily understand that "two more than three" means the same thing. In the car or at the bus stop, ask your child to help you brainstorm as many expressions for different arithmetic operations as possible; for example, "altogether," "in all," or "combined" for addition. Do *not*, however, teach these expressions as "clue words." The minute you tell your child that "more than" means "add," he will come across a question such as "How many *more than* two is five?" where he needs to subtract. Remember, above all, problem solving is about *thinking*.

➤Every now and then, pose a problem without numbers: "If you know the product of three numbers, and know two of the numbers, how can you find the third number?"

➤Challenge your child's assumptions. For example, ask, "How many squares are there in your chessboard?" Your child might quickly answer "Eight down times eight across. Sixty-four." Tell your child to look again. There are 204!

PLAN OF ATTACK

Even children who have no problem with computation can run into difficulties with word problems. Many children simply have difficulty with the *words* in a word problem. Having your child follow this plan of attack will help both of you identify your child's stumbling blocks.

1. **Read** the entire problem aloud.
2. **Say** the problem in your own words.
3. **Identify** what you've been asked to find out.
4. **List** the information you need.
5. **Estimate** a solution that would make sense.
6. **Choose** a problem-solving strategy to use.
7. **Do** the math.
8. **Check** your answer against your estimate.

➤ Whenever you come across computation problems in daily life, ask your child, "What's the best method of computation for this problem? Can you do it in your head? Do you need paper and pencil? How about a calculator? Should we make up a spreadsheet?"

HAVE MORE TIME?

➤ Play around with visual brainteasers. Many children think about math as "something you do in your head." They need practice "seeing" problems, or using their powers of visualization. Choose the visual problems in books of puzzles (see page 133), or try one of these:

• What will the next pattern of dots be?

• Can you divide this shape into four pieces that each have the same size and shape?

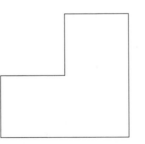

• Using only three straight lines, can you put each horse in its own pasture?

Solutions to brainteasers appear on page 174.

➤ Tell your child "If you can fold a dollar bill in half seven times, I'll give you the dollar." After your child has tried to fold the dollar, say, "Okay, answer this question and you can still have the dollar: If you *could* fold the dollar in half seven times, how many parts would it be folded into?" If your child is stumped, suggest that he use what he knows about the first few folds to create and continue a chart.

Folds	1	2	3	4	5	6	7
Parts	2	4	8	16	[32]	[64]	[128]

➤ On April Fool's Day, or any other day on which you want to point out the advantages of reading a problem carefully, give your child this brain-teaser. Then encourage him to make up similar problems to stump his friends (or enemies!).

You are the pilot of a 747 aircraft traveling at 526 miles per hour between New York and San Francisco. Three hundred sixty-one people board the plane in New York. You land in Chicago, where there is an hour and a half layover, during which 127 people get off and another 116 people get on. In Denver, there is a short 45-minute layover while 39 people get off and 81 people get on. The plane arrives in San Francisco, where everyone disembarks at 2:45 in the afternoon. What is the name of the pilot?

➤ Play Fifty. Start with 0. Take turns adding any number from 1 to 9. The person who reaches the number 50 exactly wins. At a restaurant, use any number of toothpicks or sugar packets as a starting number. Decide on a rule, such as "You can take away one, two, or three packets." The person who takes away the last toothpick wins.

These games are variations of the ancient game of Nim. See if you can play with the same rules long enough to figure out a winning strategy.

Number Sense and
Whole Number Computation

People who feel at ease with math tend to think that numbers make sense. "Well, of course numbers make sense," you might say, but it's not quite that simple. Before she ever entered school, your child probably gained the understanding that quantities get larger as numbers get bigger—that is, a group of five apples naturally is larger than a group of four apples. Now, in fifth grade, your child is asked to order the numbers ¼, ⅕, and ⅙ from least to greatest. In this case the larger number represents the *smaller* quantity. What has happened to that concept of numbers your child spent the past ten years developing? Do numbers still make sense?

Until fifth grade, your child's understanding of numbers probably developed as a result of working with whole numbers, partly because the focus of primary mathematics instruction is usually whole number computation. As your child moves into the rigorous world of fractions and decimals, however, the development of number sense once again takes the front seat. Many of the concepts your child will be learning this year aren't new. She has been working with place value at least since she started adding double-digit numbers and she has known about factors since she first studied multiplication. However, in fifth grade these concepts are given a new—and sometimes perplexing—context. Here are some of the concepts your child will be working with this year:

- Place value (for place value of decimals, see page 149)
  1. Expanded notation: $5{,}732 = 5{,}000 + 700 + 30 + 2$
  2. Exponential notation: $100 = 10 \times 10 = 10^2$
  3. Scientific notation: $5{,}732 = (5 \times 10^3) + (7 \times 10^2) + (3 \times 10) + 2$

- Number theory
  1. Prime numbers and prime factorization
  2. Multiples, including least common multiples
  3. Factors, including greatest common factor

- Properties of addition and multiplication
  1. The commutative property of addition and multiplication:
     $1 + 2 = 2 + 1 \qquad 2 \times 3 = 3 \times 2$
  2. The associative property of addition and multiplication:
     $(1 + 2) + 3 = 1 + (2 + 3) \qquad (2 \times 3) \times 4 = 2 \times (3 \times 4)$
  3. The distributive property of multiplication:
     $2 \times (3 + 7) = (2 \times 3) + (2 \times 7)$

- Order of operations
    1. Do all operations inside parentheses or brackets first.
    2. Multiply or divide in order from left to right.
    3. Add or subtract in order from left to right.

- Estimation
    1. Approximating values in computation
    2. Rounding numbers

- Positive and negative numbers

A Note About Whole Number Computation

Many teachers would like to assume that by fifth grade their students have a good grasp of addition, subtraction, multiplication, and division of whole numbers. In reality, most fifth graders still need a great deal of practice in whole number operations, especially division, with an emphasis on *using* those operations in problem-solving situations. If your child is still struggling with whole number concepts, it is imperative that you take this struggle seriously. This does *not* mean giving your child extra sheets of computation problems to complete, but rather getting to the root of her struggle and addressing it.

A Few Helpful Definitions

What is a GCF? Just in case the vocabulary of fifth grade mathematics isn't on the tip of your tongue, here's a quick cheat sheet:

Factor: A number that is multiplied. The factors of 6 are 1, 2, 3, and 6 (1 x 6 = 6; 2 x 3 = 6).

Greatest common factor (GCF): The greatest factor that two numbers have in common. The GCF of 9 and 12 is 3.

Multiple: Any product of a given number (10, 15, 20, and 100 are all multiples of 5).

Least common multiple: The smallest multiple that two numbers have in common. The LCM of 6 and 8 is 24.

Prime number: A whole number greater than 1 that has exactly two factors: 1 and itself. Examples are 2, 3, 5, 7, 11.

Prime factor: A prime number that is a factor of another number (3 is a prime factor of 12; 6 is not a prime factor of 12 because it is not a prime number).

- Ask your child's teacher *specific* questions about his difficulties and find out how to get support services if you need them.
- Give your child as much practice as possible using whole numbers to solve real-life problems.

Fifth grade math can be frightening for a child who still feels shaky about whole number operations. Your child deserves to have a solid foundation of understanding from which she can move on to the tough math ahead. Give her the time and attention she needs now, and you will never regret it.

HAVE FIVE MINUTES?

➤ Make up a passnumber. You can use a passnumber like a password to give your child entry into certain hallowed realms—the television, telephone, or computer, for example. Just don't be surprised if she turns the tables and gives *you* one for her room! Give your child everything she needs to know about the number *except* the number itself and change the number frequently to reflect topics she's currently studying in math. For example, for the number 30, you might tell your child:

- The number is between the tenth and eleventh prime numbers.
- The number has three prime factors.
- All of the number's prime factors are less than 10.

➤ Count the uncountable. Keep a hungry fifth grader occupied while you cook dinner by challenging her to come up with a method for estimating the number of grains in a box of rice. If she shrugs and says it's impossible, point out some handy kitchen measuring tools and ask her what she already knows or could easily find out. Does she know how many grams of rice the box holds? Can she find out about how many grains are in one gram? Remember, the object of the challenge is to come up with a method, not an exact answer.

➤ Play with large numbers. Is your fifth grader beginning to squirm at her eighth-grade brother's orchestra concert? Jot down a set of instructions such as these on the back of her program:

DOES SHE OR DOESN'T SHE?

How do you know if your child really understands what she's doing when she computes with whole numbers? Here are some quick ways to find out:
- Ask her to draw a picture of the problem.
- Ask her to make up a story problem that can be solved by a given computation.

- Write down the largest number you can.
- You may use each numeral only once.
- No two consecutive numbers may be next to each other.

➤Whenever your child is working on a computation problem, ask, "How many digits do you think will be in the answer?" or "Do you think the answer will be less than or greater than one thousand?"

➤Whenever you run into an interesting number—your new area code, for example, or the number on your child's football jersey—ask, "Is that a prime number? No? Then what are its factors?"

➤Point out the usefulness of negative numbers. The more firmly your child's understanding of positive and negative numbers is rooted in concrete experience, the easier working with these integers will be. Help your child gain experience by pointing out examples of negative numbers, such as
- a loss of football yardage
- degrees below zero
- feet below sea level
- a decrease of earnings

➤ Play Magic Numbers. Have your child pick a number from 2 to 9, such as 7. See how many different numbers under 100 you and your child can make using just four 7's; for example:

$$7 + 7 + 7 + 7 = 28$$
$$(7 \times 7) + (7 \times 7) = 98$$
$$[(7 \times 7) - 7] \div 7 = 6$$

➤ What's your Social Security number? Your telephone calling card number? The number on your library card, or your ATM code? Ask your child to come up with creative ways to remember important numbers; for example, "Grandma's new zip code is 54625. Hey! Five to the fourth power equals six hundred twenty-five!"

THINKING BIG

This year, your child will be expected to read and write numbers in the billions. To give her an idea of the immensity of the number, tell her that *one million* minutes equals about two years. Then help her figure out how many minutes equals *one billion* minutes (about two thousand). What a difference a few zeros make!

Divisibility Shortcuts

Your child will be figuring out "what gazinta" different numbers a lot this year in both whole number and fraction computation. To make the task easier, share these rules of divisibility.

A number is divisible by
- 2 if it is an even number.
- 3 if the sum of its digits is 3, 6, or 9.
- 4 if the last two digits are divisible by 4.
- 5 if it ends in 5 or 0.
- 6 if it is even and divisible by 3.
- 8 if the last three digits are divisible by 8.
- 9 if the sum of its digits is 9.
- 10 if it ends in 0.

To find the sum of a number's digits, keep adding until you get to a single digit. To get the digital sum for 764, for example, add 7 + 6 + 4 = 17, then add 1 + 7 = 8.

HAVE MORE TIME?

➤ On your next grocery shopping trip, give your child the grocery list and ask, "How much do you think we will spend?" As you shop, ask your child to keep an approximate running total in her head and to let you know when she thinks you've reached her original estimate. Finally, see how close your actual total comes to her original estimate and her approximate total.

➤ Create a birthday factor tree. A factor tree (which can go up or down) is a graphic way of listing all the prime factors in any given number. For example, a factor tree for the number 12 might look like this:

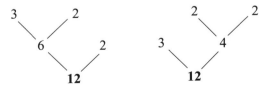

For a birthday factor tree, start with the month and day of your child's birthday in numbers. For example, June 10 would be 6-10, or 610. Have your child create the number's factor tree on a sheet of large white paper and draw a tree design around the tree. Create a tree for each family member and compare trees. Who has the most branches? How about the least?

➤ Introduce your child to the Sieve of Eratosthenes. The Greek astronomer Eratosthenes invented this method for finding prime numbers in 200 B.C., and it is still used today. Here are the directions.

1. Ask your child to make a hundred chart as shown.
2. Cross out the number 1. One is not a prime number.
3. Leave the number 2. It is a prime number. Cross out all multiples of 2 (even numbers), because they are not prime.
4. Following the same procedure, leave these numbers but cross out their multiples: 3, 5, 7.
5. Any number not crossed out is a prime number.

1	2	3	4	5	6	7	8	9	10
11	12	13	14	15	16	17	18	19	20
21	22	23	24	25	26	27	28	29	30
31	32	33	34	35	36	37	38	39	40
41	42	43	44	45	46	47	48	49	50
51	52	53	54	55	56	57	58	59	60
61	62	63	64	65	66	67	68	69	70
71	72	73	74	75	76	77	78	79	80
81	82	83	84	85	86	87	88	89	90
91	92	93	94	95	96	97	98	99	100

➤ Make a place value chart. Even children who have a pretty good grasp of place value can get confused by the new ways of writing numbers that they learn in fifth grade. To help keep the numbers straight, suggest that your child make a place value chart like the one below and tape it to the front of her math notebook.

hundred trillions / ten trillions / trillions / hundred billions / ten billions / billions / hundred millions / ten millions / millions / hundred thousands / ten thousands / thousands / hundreds / tens / ones

➤ Play Operation War. Here's how:

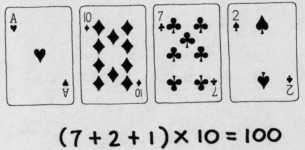

OPERATION WAR

1. Remove the face cards from a deck of cards.
2. Deal out four cards to each person.
3. Players try to combine the cards to make 100, following these rules.
   • They must use all four cards.
   • They can use the cards in any order.
   • They can use any operation and grouping system.
4. The player who gets closest to, but not over, 100 wins the round.

$$(7 + 2 + 1) \times 10 = 100$$

Eureka!

Fractions

Many fifth graders' (and their parents') difficulty with mathematics can be summed up in just three words: fear of fractions. Even for a fifth grader who made it through long division without a hitch, fractions come as a shock to the system. For one thing, fractions don't behave at all like whole numbers. Multiply two whole numbers and you get a larger number, but multiply two fractions and you get a *smaller* number. Where's the sense in *that*? Fractions are also slippery. One third of my jumbo candy bar does not equal one third of your mini candy bar. On the other hand, you tell me that one third equals two sixths, three ninths, and four twelfths. Is it any wonder that generation after generation of students throws up its hands in exasperation and lives by the old saw "Mine is not to reason why, just invert and multiply."

Life with fractions can be tough. But it doesn't have to be. The main reason working with fractions is so difficult for many fifth graders is that they don't really have a good sense of what a fraction is. Try this experiment. Draw the following number line on a sheet of paper. Then ask your child to place the number ⅓ on the number line.

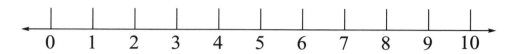

If your child placed ⅓ between 0 and 1, you are lucky. Somewhere along the line, your child has had enough concrete experience in fractions to understand the basic concept that ⅓ is less than 1. If, on the other hand, your child could not place the fraction correctly, do not despair. Rather, commit yourself to providing the background in fraction concepts that your child is missing. You can do this by

- Using concrete materials such as fraction strips (see page 205) or pattern blocks whenever your child is working with fractions.
- Reviewing the vocabulary and symbols of fractions.
- Playing around with equivalent fractions.

Finding the equivalents for different fractions—"renaming" fractions—is fundamental to all computation work with fractions. Do not try to teach your child specific methods of fraction computation. Your methods are likely to differ from your child's teacher's, which would lead to confusion and frustration for everyone. Instead, focus on activities that will strengthen your child's understanding of fraction equivalents. The more adept your child is at renaming fractions, the easier the actual computation work will be.

HAVE FIVE MINUTES?

➤ Enlist your child's help in the kitchen. Cooking is one of the few activities in which we use fractions on a daily basis. To add a bit of challenge:
  - Ask your child to double or halve a recipe.
  - "Lose" all but the ¼- or ⅓-cup measure and see if your child can figure out how to come up with the amounts he needs.
  - Suggest that your child create a recipe of his own and record it with exact measurements.

➤ Ask, "What fraction of your day do you spend sleeping? How much of your day does that leave for other things?" You can ask the same question about watching television, eating, doing homework, and so on. Do the fractions add up to one whole day?

➤Any time you are measuring with your child (see page 159), ask questions such as the ones below. Allow your child to work out his own method for coming up with the answer.

- "How many ¼-inch segments are there in 3 inches?" [3 ÷ ¼ = 12]
- "What is ½ of 3¾ feet?" [½ x 3 ¾ = 1⅞]
- "What part of a foot is 8 inches?" [8/12 or ⅔]

➤Talk about people fractions. While you're waiting in line at the grocery store, ask, "What fraction of people in this line are wearing blue jeans?" Have your child give his answer in lowest terms.

➤Find fractions in the news. Ask your child to look through the newspaper or a magazine and circle any fractions he finds. Choose one fraction, such as "⅓ off," and ask your child to give you an example of what the fraction means.

The Language of Fractions

Fractions have their own vocabulary, which is often deceiving. For instance, why do we talk about "reducing" or "simplifying" a fraction if the actual size of the fraction stays the same? You might want to check this list when the going gets tough.

Parts of a fraction:

numerator (number of parts being considered)

denominator (number of total parts)

Proper fraction: The number on the bottom is larger than the number on the top. ¾

Improper fraction: The number on the top is larger than the number on the bottom. 5/4

Mixed numeral: A whole number accompanied by a fraction. 1¼

Lowest terms (reduce, simplify): 4/8 = ½

Least common denominator (LCD): For ⅓ and ¼, the LCD is 12 because 12 is the smallest multiple that 3 and 4 have in common.

Least common multiple, greatest common factor: See page 139.

Of ("Of" means "times"): ⅖ of 20 = ⅖ × 20 = 8

Invert (inverse): The inverse of ¾ is 4/3.

➤ Keep track of what fraction of the school year is over, stated—of course—in lowest terms.

➤ Play Name a Fraction. Any time you have a few minutes to kill, see how many fractions your child can name
   • that come between ¼ and ½.
   • that come between 2 and 3.
   • whose sum is 1.
   • whose product is between ½ and 1.

HAVE MORE TIME?

➤ Make fraction models. Suggest that your child make his own paper models by tracing around a bowl (for pie-shaped fractions) or a book (for rectangular-shaped fractions), and cutting out the shape. Have him fold the shape into halves, quarters, and eighths; or thirds, sixths, and twelfths. The folding process itself will reinforce the concept of equivalent fractions.

➤ Play Hit the Target. Write a fraction, such as 3⅛, on a sheet of paper and post it on the refrigerator door. See how many different ways family members can rename the fraction in the course of the day or week. For example, it can be written as ²⁴⁄₈ + ⅛, ²⁵⁄₈, 2⅝, ⅛ of 25, and so on.

➤ Play Fraction Trade-In. Make two copies of the fraction strips on page 207 and cut the strips apart. Then follow these rules:

FRACTION TRADE-IN

1. Use only the following strips: 1, $\frac{1}{2}$, $\frac{1}{4}$, $\frac{1}{8}$, $\frac{1}{16}$.
2. Each player begins with a 1 strip. Place one $\frac{1}{2}$, one $\frac{1}{4}$, one $\frac{1}{8}$, and one $\frac{1}{16}$ in a paper bag. Then place the rest of the strips in the center of the table.
3. Players take turns drawing a strip from the bag. They then exchange their strips so that their strips have the correct denominator and turn one in to the center. For example, a player starts with 1 and draws $\frac{1}{4}$. He may exchange his 1 strip for four $\frac{1}{4}$ strips and turn one of them in.
4. The first player to turn in all his strips wins.
5. For variety, try playing with different combinations of strips or with two or more wholes.

➤ Play Fraction War. You can vary this game according to the specific skills your child is studying at the time. Here's how.

FRACTION WAR 1

1. Use only ace–10 in a deck of cards. Aces equal one.
2. Deal all the cards so that each player has the same number. Discard any cards left over.
3. Each player turns over two cards and makes a fraction. For example, a 3 and a 7 can make either $^3/_7$ or $^7/_3$.
4. The player with the largest fraction takes both cards from all players.
5. The player with the most cards at the end of the game wins.

FRACTION WAR 2

1. Follow steps 1, 2, and 3 above.
2. Players record the fractions they make on a sheet of paper.
3. Players continue to repeat the previous steps, adding the fractions they record.
4. The player with the largest fraction at the end of the game wins.

FRACTION WARS 3, 4, 5

1. Follow the steps for Fraction War 2.
2. For Fraction War 3, players subtract the smaller fraction from the larger one each time they record a fraction. The player with the *smallest* fraction wins.
3. For Fraction War 4, players multiply the fractions they record. The player with the *smallest* fraction wins.
4. For Fraction War 5, players divide the fractions they record. The player with the *largest* fraction wins.

➤ Use a graph to find equivalent fractions. Help your child draw a graph like the one shown on the next page. Draw a line from 0 through the point (5, 10). Point to the point (5, 10) and ask, "If this point represents $^5/_{10}$, how do you think you can find some fractions equivalent to $^5/_{10}$?" Show your child how the equivalent fractions can be found at other points of intersection along the line.

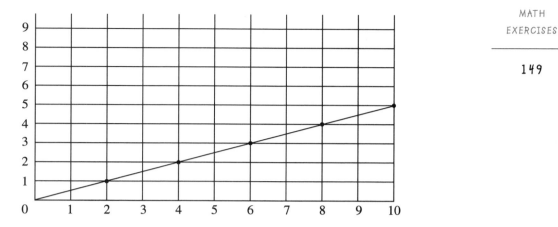

➤ Make up fraction puzzles. Have your child use two glasses and water to figure out the puzzle below. Then have him make up a puzzle to try to stump you!

Start with one full glass of water. Pour out half. Then pour half of what you poured out back in. Pour out a third of what you now have. Then pour back in a third of a glass. What fraction of the glass is now full of water? [⅚]

Decimals

Not too long ago, a fifth grader didn't have to worry much about decimals. Traditional curricula dictated the instruction of fractions in fifth grade, decimals in sixth. Times have changed, however. Calculators, computers, and increased use of the metric system (and don't forget money!) have made decimals a part of everyday life.

Working with decimals should be a natural extension of working with fractions (in fact, decimals *are* fractions) and whole numbers (they follow the same place value system). Why, then, do they cause such problems—even for adults?

It's all because of that pesky decimal point. (Is that $100.04 that you owe on your taxes or $10,004?) The methods for computing with decimals are remarkably similar to those for computing with whole numbers. The problem is what to do with that decimal point. Your child can memorize all the "count the decimal places" rules she's given, but unless she has a

IN CASE YOU FORGOT . . .

Here is a brief rundown of fraction computation.

Addition $\frac{2}{3} + \frac{1}{5} = \frac{10}{15} + \frac{3}{15} = \frac{13}{15}$
$1\frac{1}{4} + 2\frac{1}{3} = \frac{5}{4} + \frac{7}{3} = \frac{15}{12} + \frac{28}{12} = \frac{43}{12} = 3\frac{7}{12}$

Subtraction $\frac{5}{6} - \frac{1}{4} = \frac{10}{12} - \frac{3}{12} = \frac{7}{12}$

Multiplication $\frac{5}{8} \times \frac{2}{3} = \frac{10}{24} = \frac{5}{12}$
$1\frac{1}{4} \times 1\frac{1}{2} = \frac{5}{4} \times \frac{3}{2} = \frac{15}{8} = 1\frac{7}{8}$

Division $\frac{7}{8} \div \frac{1}{2} = \frac{7}{8} \times \frac{2}{1} = 1\frac{6}{8} = 1\frac{3}{4}$

good understanding of what decimals are and how they work, she will never know if where she finally puts that decimal point actually makes sense.

You can help your child make sense of decimals through activities that emphasize the following concepts:

- A decimal is a fraction. The decimal point shows where the whole number ends and the fraction begins.
  - All decimals can be written as fractions and all fractions can be written as decimals.
  - The decimal place value system is an extension of the base-ten system for whole numbers. Each place in a number is ten times the value of the place to its right.
  - Computation methods for decimals are exactly like those for whole numbers, except that you must keep track of the decimal points. Estimating the size of the answer will help you know if you have kept track correctly.

TRICKS OF THE TRADE

One of the beauties of the decimal place value system is that it is just like our whole number system. In fact, it is the same system: base ten. This means that each place in a number is ten times the value of the place to its right (or, conversely, one tenth the value of the place to its left). When working with decimals, an understanding of place value translates into a nifty trick:

- To multiply by a power of ten (10, 100, 1,000), move the decimal point to the *right* the number of zeros in the multiplier:
  - 4.3578 x 10 = 43.578
  - 4.3578 x 100 = 435.78
  - 4.3578 x 1,000 = 4,357.8
- To divide by a power of ten (10, 100, 1,000), move the decimal point in the decimal to the *left* the number of zeros in the divisor:
  - 687.4 ÷ 10 = 68.74
  - 687.4 ÷ 100 = 6.874
  - 687.4 ÷ 1,000 = .6874

HAVE FIVE MINUTES?

➤ Point out and talk about the meaning of the decimals that you come across in your daily life: prices, odometer readings, sports statistics, and temperature and other measurements.

➤ Use money to demonstrate decimal concepts. When your child is totaling the contents of her piggy bank for the hundredth time, ask for the total. Then ask,
- "How many whole dollars are in that total?"
- "How many tenths of a dollar are there?"
- "How many hundredths?"
- "Why is the decimal point there?" [to separate the whole dollars from the fractions of a dollar]

➤ Play with license plate numbers. In the car or walking along the street, point out a license plate number. Use that number (minus any letters) to give your child practice in decimal values and vocabulary. For the license number 546 M83, you might ask:

- "What are the smallest and largest numbers you can make with that number?" [.54683 and 54,683]
- "What number can you make that falls between 54 and 55?" [54.683]
- "What number would be rounded off to 5,000?" [5468.3]

➤ Compute gas mileage. Put your child in charge of figuring out gas mileage on a long trip. Point out how to read the odometer and number of gallons on the gas pump, but leave it to her to find a way to figure out the mileage itself.

➤ Ask your child to help you find unit prices at the grocery store by dividing the price of a purchase by the unit of measure. For example, if a five-pound bag of apples costs $2.89, you would divide 2.89 by 5 to find the unit price. This is also a good time to talk about rounding. Ask, "What can you do to $2.89 to make it easier to work with?" [Change it to $2.90 or even $3.00.]

➤ Help your child start a bank account of her own. If she already has a bank account, talk about other ways she might want to consider investing her money. Many banks have excellent programs for fledgling investors.

➤ Convert on the calculator. What is ⅛ expressed as a decimal? Remind your child that the fraction bar in a fraction means the same as "divided by." Punch 1 ÷ 8 into a calculator. Presto! You've got an answer. Choose a fraction and, without doing any calculations, estimate its decimal equivalent. Then have your child find the decimal notation on the calculator. Whose estimate was closest?

HAVE MORE TIME?

➤ Need something to keep an active mind occupied on a rainy day? Get out the spare change jar, use your child's old play money, or suggest that your child make a set of paper pennies, dimes, and nickels. Then draw a four-by-four grid on a sheet of paper and present this challenge: "Use pennies, dimes, and dollars. Make every row going down and going across equal the same amount."

➤ Make a copy of page 206 and mark off a 10 x 10 square block. Invite your child to make a pattern by coloring in different squares. When your child has finished the pattern, ask, "What part of this picture is colored red?" (say, twenty-eight squares or ²⁸⁄₁₀₀). Help her record the number in decimal notation (.28). Do the same for the other colors in the pattern. For an added challenge, suggest that your child make another pattern using the same proportions, for example, .30 red, .25 yellow, and .15 blue.

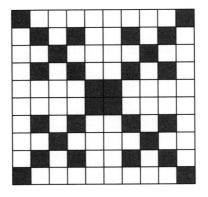

➤ Play Challenge the Calculator. You need a calculator for this game. Here are the rules:

CHALLENGE THE CALCULATOR

1. Ask your child to find ten decimal numbers in a newspaper or reference book and write the numbers on slips of paper. Place the slips facedown on a table.
2. Turn over one slip at a time. To gain a point, your child must round each decimal to the nearest *whole number* and say it aloud before you can display the original number on the calculator. For example, suppose you turn over the number 367.987. Your child rounds the number to the nearest whole and shouts "368!" Meanwhile, you have managed to input the numbers 367.98 . . . Your child wins that round.
3. The player with the most points at the end of ten rounds wins.

➤ Give your child control of her own purse strings. There is no better way to understand the power of the decimal point than to have to keep track of your own money! Whether you choose to give your child an allowance, pay her for household chores, or help her brainstorm other ways to earn money, the hands-on experience of handling her own money will give your child a leg up in working with decimals as well as a whole range of valuable life skills.

➤ Encourage your child to start her own business. The entrepreneurial spirit of most fifth graders rivals that of Donald Trump. (Why do you think Girl Scout cookie sales are such a success?) The best ideas will most likely come from your child, but if you need some help, check out one of these books in your library or bookstore.

- *Making Cents: Every Kid's Guide to Money: How to Make It, What to Do with It,* by Elizabeth Wilkinson (Little, Brown)
- *The Kid's Guide to Money: Earning It, Saving It, Spending It, Growing It, Sharing It,* by Steve Otfinoski (Scholastic)
- *Jobs for Kids: The Guide to Having Fun and Making Money,* by Carol Barkin (Lothrop, Lee and Shepard)

Neatness Counts

If your child is having a hard time with decimal computation, it could be that her numbers are going astray. Here are some suggestions for helping her stay on course:

- Use graph paper for computation work.
- Turn notebook paper sideways and write the numbers in columns.
- Make a place value grid like the one shown.

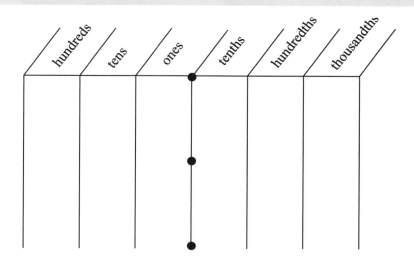

Geometry

Ah, for the days of shapes and sizes! Every parent remembers pointing out circles, squares, and triangles to a child: "You're right! That's a *circle*! Very good!" Those were joyful days, filled with discovery and growth. You could practically *see* the wheels turning in your child's mind.

But now your child is in fifth grade, bringing home pages of definitions and formulas. Where is the joy? Where are the wheels turning?

Never fear, the wheels are still turning. Certainly the method of study has become more formal and systematic. No toddler ever had to describe the properties of a square. Yet, the same skills your toddler used in figuring out the difference between a square and a triangle are at work as your fifth grader figures out the characteristics of a polygon.

Geometric concepts are among the first mathematical concepts your child learns, and they continue to be among the most important. Try following a map, planning a visual presentation, or playing a game of baseball without using geometry. In the past, geometry has been slighted in many math curricula—an "extra" to be studied at the end of the year, only after the "real" work of arithmetic computation was completed. In recent years, however, educators have begun placing more emphasis on the importance of spatial concepts in mathematical reasoning. In the primary grades, children develop an intuitive understanding of geometric ideas by drawing, cutting, folding, and flipping shapes. These types of activities are still the best way to reinforce your child's understanding of the more advanced geometric principles, such as area and perimeter, that he will be learning this year. By pointing out the geometry you use every time you help your child mark off a basketball court or decorate a room for a birthday party, you will strengthen your child's ability to think spatially. And you'll both have fun in the process!

HAVE FIVE MINUTES?

➤ Play with shadows. Turn out the lights and hold up various three-dimensional objects (small boxes and canned goods work well) in front of a flashlight to make shadows on the wall. Talk about the relationship between the three-dimensional object and its two-dimensional shadow. Does the shape of the shadow change if you hold the object differently?

➤ What did the obtuse angle say to the acute angle? (How about "O U Q T?") To review geometry vocabulary, make up conversations between geometric elements. Take the part of one element, have your child take the part of another, and spend a few moments touting each other's (or your own) virtues.

➤ Let your child be the navigator. Wherever you are going—across town, across the mall, or across the United States—encourage your child to find the destination on a map and plot a route for getting there. Map reading gives your child practice in using coordinate geometry and in understanding spatial relationships.

➤ Cut the cards. Give your child an index card and a pair of scissors. Ask, "Can you make one cut and move one piece to turn this rectangle into a parallelogram?" Encourage your child to use the pieces to form other shapes. Each time your child creates a new shape, ask, "Did the total area of the card change?" [No] This experience will help prepare your child for working with area (see Measurement, page 159).

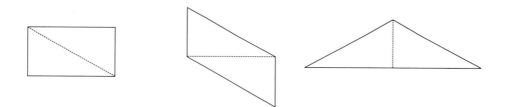

➤ Design a polygon alphabet. Any time you have a few minutes to kill and a paper and pencil handy, challenge your child to see how many letters he can make using only polygons. Be sure to remind him that polygons have no curves—and they also have no holes!

ABCDEFGH

➤ Curl and cut. Are you trying to make dinner with a surprisingly large, hungry fifth grader hanging around the kitchen? To get you-know-who out from under your feet, hand him a stack of recycled paper and a pair of scissors. Suggest that he roll a strip of paper into a cylinder, cut into the edges or rolled sides, and unroll it. What happens? (It makes a repeating symmetrical design.) Ask, "What are some other ways you can roll the paper?" See how many different roll-and-cut designs he can make while you finish preparing dinner.

HAVE MORE TIME?

➤ Copy a design. Have your child draw a geometric design on the back of a paper place mat or on any sheet of paper. Without looking at the design, try to draw a duplicate by following the directions your child gives you. Then switch roles and find out for yourself how difficult the task of giving clear directions really is!

➤ Buy your child a protractor and compass, and let him experiment with constructing different kinds of shapes. Show him how to make patterns such as the following. Then challenge him to come up with patterns of his own.

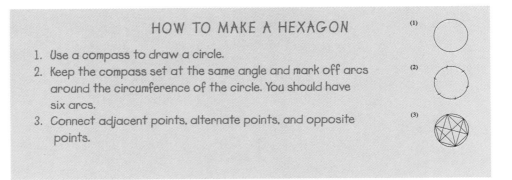

HOW TO MAKE A HEXAGON

1. Use a compass to draw a circle.
2. Keep the compass set at the same angle and mark off arcs around the circumference of the circle. You should have six arcs.
3. Connect adjacent points, alternate points, and opposite points.

(1)
(2)
(3)

➤ Have an angle scavenger hunt. Got a long, rainy afternoon and a restless fifth grader? Extend a protractor by taping one end of a foot-long piece of string to the back and threading the other end through the hole in the center as shown. Have him use the protractor to measure angles in household features such as wallpaper and windowpanes. Give your child a list of different kinds of angles to find—for example, acute, obtuse, 45°, right, 75°, and so on—or ask him to find as many examples of one type of angle as he can.

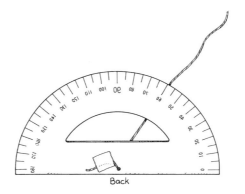

Back

➤ Make a marshmallow structure. If that rainy afternoon turns into a rainy weekend, try giving your child a handful of toothpicks and miniature marshmallows. Show him how to stick the toothpicks into the marshmallows to make constructions. Challenge him to make as many different geometric shapes as he can *before* he gobbles down the marshmallows. (For a more tooth-friendly version of this activity, you can use bits of clay instead of marshmallows.)

➤ Try the index card challenge. Give your child a stack of index cards and a pair of scissors and challenge him to build the tallest structure he can. Here's the catch: He may cut and fold the cards in any way, but he may not use tape, staples, or any other adhesives.

➤ Introduce your child to the fine art of *wycinanki* (vi-chee-NON-kee), or Polish cut-paper designs. Fold a sheet of construction paper in half and ask your child to draw *half* of a design, keeping in mind that the fold in the paper will be the center of the design. Remind your child that the more cuts he makes, the more intricate the design will be.

➤ Play around with tangrams. Trace the pattern below onto a piece of poster board. (Or, for a sturdier version, cut the individual pieces out of recycled plastic lids.) Have your child cut the pieces apart. Ask your child to use all seven pieces to make each of these polygons: square, rectangle, parallelogram, trapezoid. Then ask him to use only the triangles to make a trapezoid, a pentagon, and a hexagon. After your child has mastered these puzzles, suggest that he make up challenges for *you* to solve.

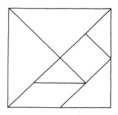

Oh, That's a Whatchamacallit!

If it's been a while since the last time you used the word *rhombus* or *trapezoid,* here are a few quick reminders.

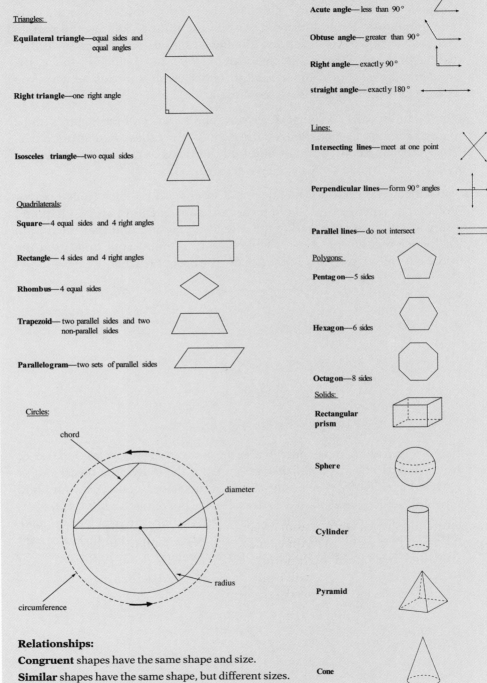

Triangles:

Equilateral triangle—equal sides and equal angles

Right triangle—one right angle

Isosceles triangle—two equal sides

Quadrilaterals:

Square—4 equal sides and 4 right angles

Rectangle— 4 sides and 4 right angles

Rhombus—4 equal sides

Trapezoid— two parallel sides and two non-parallel sides

Parallelogram—two sets of parallel sides

Circles:

chord

diameter

radius

circumference

Angles:

Acute angle—less than 90°

Obtuse angle—greater than 90°

Right angle—exactly 90°

straight angle—exactly 180°

Lines:

Intersecting lines—meet at one point

Perpendicular lines—form 90° angles

Parallel lines—do not intersect

Polygons:

Pentagon—5 sides

Hexagon—6 sides

Octagon—8 sides

Solids:

Rectangular prism

Sphere

Cylinder

Pyramid

Cone

Relationships:

Congruent shapes have the same shape and size.
Similar shapes have the same shape, but different sizes.

➤ Play Coordinate Tic-tac-toe. You need graph paper or a copy of page 206 and two sets of markers, such as buttons, coins, or slips of paper with X's and O's written on them. Here's how to play.

COORDINATE TIC-TAC-TOE

1. Draw a coordinate graph like the one shown.
2. The game is played just like Tic-tac-toe, except that the X's and O's are placed at points of intersection instead of in spaces.
3. Players take turns naming the point where they want to place their markers. For example, you say "three, two" and place your marker on the intersection of 3 and 2—written (3,2). Your child then says "five, four" and places his marker on (5, 4).
4. Play continues until one player has placed four markers in a row.

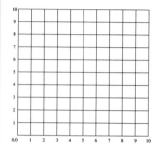

Measurement

Your child has been using measurement concepts since she was very small: "Big truck!" "I want *that* [the largest] cookie!" Most children love to measure. From plastic buckets full of sand (volume) to their first "real" watch (time), many of their favorite toys were actually tools of measurement.

Much of your child's instruction in measurement during her primary years probably involved using measuring tools—rulers, scales, measuring cups, clocks, thermometers, and so on. In the upper grades, measurement is often used as a vehicle for computation instruction: "Jane has a piece of board that is 2¼ feet long. How long will each piece be if she saws the board in half?" or "The Empire State Building is 381 meters tall. How tall is it in centimeters?" This year, your child's work with customary and metric units of measure for length, capacity, weight, mass, elapsed time, and temperature will most likely focus on converting and computing with units within the same system of measure. If she hasn't done so already, she will begin a formal study of area, perimeter, and volume, and she will be introduced to formulas for each.

In short, measurement just got hard. To complicate matters, most fifth graders simply are not developmentally ready to work on the abstract level required for following conversion rules and formulas. Strong math programs give plenty of hands-on experience in estimating, measuring, and comparing measures to bridge the gap between concrete and abstract understanding.

Even if your child is not getting these kinds of experiences at school, you can help by making sure she has plenty of "real world" measuring experiences at home. Luckily, measurement is already an integral part of your daily routine. When do you need to leave for work? Do you have enough gas to get there? Will last night's leftover spaghetti fit in your plastic lunch container? If you think about it, you will find that you are constantly using measurement as a problem-solving tool. All you have to do is invite your child to share the experience.

Measurement Sense

Often, what people call common sense is actually measurement sense. When you ask your child in exasperation, "Did you *really* think you were going to fit all your library books in that backpack?" you are commenting on her sense of volume. Measurement sense, like common sense, is gained through experience. To help build your child's sense of measurement, it might help to keep these three important concepts in mind.

1. Different measures serve different purposes. To find out if that cooler will fit in the trunk of the car, you need to know its *length, width,* and *height.* The same dimensions might help you decide how many cans of soda the cooler will hold, but not until you have multiplied them together to find its *volume.*

2. Different *units* of measure serve different purposes. Yards might be best for measuring the distance between bus stops, but miles are better for the distance between towns.

3. All measures are approximations. The "sense" in measurement sense is the ability to judge just how approximate the measure needs to be. "About ten yards" might work fine for a game of touch football, but not for the Super Bowl!

HAVE FIVE MINUTES?

➤ Sort by measure. The next time you are pulling dirty laundry out from under your child's bed or sorting through mismatched gloves, make two piles. Ask, "Which pile is bigger?" Talk about how your child reached her conclusion. By height? By weight? By the number of items in the pile? Would her answer change if you laid the items in each pile end to end and measured their length?

➤ Looking for a dinner table topic? Ask, "Suppose an alien wanted to make an exact replica of our home. What are some ways we could describe it?" After you have exhausted the obvious—number and size of rooms, height of ceilings, area of front yard, and so on—move to the not-so-obvious. How about the surface area covered by rugs? The number of doorknobs? The total volume of the closets?

Inch by Inch or Centimeter by Centimeter?

Ours is not a simple world. At the grocery store, your flour is measured in customary units (pounds) while your soda comes by the liter (metric units). In school, your child is probably studying two systems of measurement as well. And—in the United States at least—she will probably continue to use both systems throughout her life. What's a parent to do? Ask your child or her teacher which system she is currently studying at school, but *do not attempt to teach your child how to convert from one system to the other.* Instead, supply her with as many tools for measuring in both systems as you can afford, and give her plenty of experience using those tools as often as possible.

Handy measurement tools to have around include:
- a ruler with both inches and centimeter marks
- a yardstick
- a meter stick
- a tape measure
- measuring spoons
- a bathroom scale
- a balance scale with metric weights
- a thermometer with both Fahrenheit and Celsius scales

➤ Ask, "Can you find something in the house that has a perimeter of about three feet? How can you prove it?" Remind your child that *perimeter* is the distance around the *rim* of the object.

➤ Pack in the volume. Whether you are packing a suitcase or a grocery bag or a cardboard carton full of basement junk, talk about the container's contents in terms of volume: "What is the volume of this drawer in T-shirts?" or "How many soda cans fit in this box? What is its volume in cans?" Volume is a difficult concept for a lot of fifth graders, probably because it involves translating two-dimensional properties (length, width, and height) into a three-dimensional measure. The more informal experience your child has with the notion that volume measures three-dimensional space, the easier the more abstract work with formulas will be.

➤ Measure an egg. Need to occupy your child while the banana bread is baking? Hold up an egg and ask, "How many ways can you measure an egg?" List all the ways you can think of (length, circumference, weight, volume of the shell, liquid-ounce measure of the raw egg . . .). Then see if your child can devise methods for obtaining each of the measures.

➤ What's in a year? Ask, "How many weeks are in a year? How many days?" Then ask, "How many pages of homework equal one year? How many soccer games?" Challenge your child to come up with her own ways to measure one year.

➤ Put your kitchen in order. When your child is helping you cook or (dream on) clean out the cupboards, hand her three or four items, such as a bag of nuts, a bottle of vanilla, and a sugar bowl. Ask her to place the items in order by weight (or, using metric units, mass). If you have a kitchen scale, check her order against the items' actual weight.

➤ What's the fastest route to school? Does the school bus, city bus, or your car take the fastest route? Give your child a city map and have her plan two different routes to school. If possible, try out both routes. Is the shortest route necessarily the fastest? What factors contribute to how long it takes her to get to school?

➤ Play with conversions. Tell your child, "Our gasoline tank holds twenty-five gallons of gas. You drink about one twelve-ounce soda a day. How many gasoline tankfuls of soda do you drink in a year?" The *Guinness Book of World Records* is a great resource for this kind of activity. Most fifth graders adore the wild trivia and love comparing the fantastic feats in the book to their own benchmarks.

➤ Ask, "What unit of measure would you use to measure this room? Can you think of a reason why you might use a different unit of measure? What about a spoonful of water?"

HAVE MORE TIME?

➤ Find benchmarks. Most of the measuring people do each day takes the form of estimating. The better a person is at "eyeballing" certain measures, the easier it is to get along in life. Experiment with your child to help her come up with benchmarks that make sense to her. Does the width of one of her fingers equal a centimeter? Is there another part of her body that's close to a foot? How many gallons does the bathtub or sink hold? What common object weighs just about a pound?

➤ Make a balance scale. Give your child a pile of recycled containers and craft materials and challenge her to make a working scale. Once she has the scale functioning to her satisfaction, see if she can use it to come up with a standard of measure by weighing small objects against the same units. How much does your watch weigh in paper clips?

➤Find playing card area. The next time you are playing cards, ask, "How many playing cards do you think would cover the surface of this table [this book, this rug, that wall]? How can we find out? Now, suppose we sawed the table in half diagonally. How many playing cards would cover one of the triangles we made?"

➤Ask, "How many miles [or kilometers] do you think you will walk tomorrow?" Help your child come up with a way to figure out the answer.

➤Make an indoor (or outdoor) miniature golf course. Suggest that your child use anything she can find—cardboard boxes, furniture, coffee cans, Frisbees—to make obstacles for the course. The course may be set up in any way your child wants as long as its total length matches a distance that you give her. When she has completed her course, use a wrapping paper tube or a yardstick and a ball of aluminum foil to have your own mini Masters tournament.

➤Make a musical instrument. Have your child experiment with filling different-sized glasses or glass bottles to various levels and tapping them with the end of a spoon. Have her place the glasses in order to make a "scale" of lowest to highest notes. Talk about the results. Does the height of liquid in the glasses affect the sound? (Not necessarily.) What does? (The capacity or amount of water in each glass.) For more ideas on making musical instruments and other crafts that involve measurement, check out these or other craft books in your library or bookstore.
  • *Making Music: 6 Instruments You Can Create,* by Eddie Herschel Oates (Harpercrest)
  • *Making Things,* by Ann Wiseman (Little, Brown)
  • *Rubber-Band Banjos and a Java-Jive Bass: Projects and Activities on the Science of Music and Sound,* by Alex Sabbeth (John Wiley and Sons)
  • *World Crafts: Musical Instruments,* by Meryl Doney (Franklin Watts)

Ratio and Percent

Many parents are surprised to learn that ratio and percent actually *aren't* "new topics." They are merely different ways of talking about good old fractions and decimals. Take the fraction ½. By fifth grade, most children know instinctively that ½ and 50% are the same thing—that an item marked "50% off" at a store is half-price. They also know that ½ can equal .50—that half a dollar equals $0.50. So they are aware that ½, 0.50, and 50% are just different names for the same number.

Any child who has checked out the speedometer on a car or read a highway speed limit sign also instinctively knows something about rate. Rates are comparisons, often expressed in fraction notation: "55 miles in 1 hour" is commonly written "55 mi/hr." Percentages, too, are rates that tell how many *per* one hundred.

Ratios can be combined into statements of equality called proportions: ½ = 50/100 is a proportion. It might be useful to think of proportions as pairs of relationships (1 is to 2 as 50 is to 100) or as equivalent fractions.

Math programs rarely introduce ratios and percents before fifth grade. You can help your child make sense of these concepts by building on what he already knows. For example, if he knows that a 50% discount means half off, would 25% be more or less than that? By how much? Once you start talking about percents and ratios, you will be amazed at how much your child already knows—and how ready he is to learn.

HAVE FIVE MINUTES?

➤ Hunt for percents. Give your child a newspaper or news magazine and ask, "How many percents can you find in five minutes?" Have him highlight or cut out each example. Then, choose one example and ask your child to explain what the percent means in its context.

➤ Is it reasonable? Watch commercials and look through ads to find uses of percents or ratios, then talk about whether the numbers make sense. If, for example, a local store advertises "Rock bottom prices! Everything 15% off!" ask your child, "Do you think 15% is rock bottom? Why or why not?" You can also manufacture statements of your own: "There must be ten articles about men for every one article about women in this issue of *Sports Illustrated!* What do *you* think?"

PLAYING BY THE RULES

Sometime this year, your child might come home with formulas for measuring area and volume. These formulas might look vaguely familiar, or they might look like Greek to you (which is exactly what π is in the formula for the area of a circle!). Here is a list of some of the more common formulas your child might be studying. Do not attempt to teach these formulas to your child; rather, focus your energies on experiences that will give her a firm understanding of the *ideas* behind the formulas. Remember, a shortcut is only good if you know where you're going.

Some common abbreviations:

b = base h = height
l = length w = width
r = radius
π = pi, an irrational number approximately equal to 3.14

Formulas:

Area of a rectangle = $l \times w$ (or $b \times h$)
Area of a triangle = $\frac{1}{2}(b \times h)$
Area of a circle = πr^2

➤ Figure out the tip. Choose an occasion when you have plenty of time after a restaurant meal and hand the task of tipping to your child. Tell your child the amount of the check and the percent of that amount that you wish to tip. If your child is stumped, work with what he knows. Does he know what 10% of the bill would be? If so, what could he do to that number to get to 15% or 20%?

➤ Comparison shop. Which is a better deal, a $15 magazine subscription at 5% off or a $20 magazine subscription at 20% off? You might find that your fifth grader is a surprisingly astute shopper, especially when his own money is involved.

➤ Get into the habit of asking "What ratio does that make?" or "What percent is that?" If your child tells you that fifteen out of the twenty kids in his class eat a hot lunch, ask, "What would be a simpler way to talk about that ratio?" [3 to 4] or "What percentage of kids would that be?" [75%].

➤ Use percents and ratios in financial negotiations. Any time you pay your child for an odd job or give your child an allowance increase, use the language of ratios and percents:

- "I'll pay you $3 per hour or a flat fee of $10 for looking after your brother during the meeting. Which do you prefer?"
- "I got a 5% raise in my salary this year, so I think a 5% raise in your allowance is fair. What do you think?"
- "If you pay 75% for that new pair of skates, I'll pitch in the remaining 25%."

➤ Use ratios to organize your child's time. If your fifth grader tells you, "I'll *never* get this homework finished!" respond with a mathematical solution: "Okay, it took you fifteen minutes to write a half a page. How long do you think it will take you to write a whole page?"

A RATIO CHEAT SHEET

Few people get through the day without doing some "proportional thinking," but many don't know the formal terms for what they're doing. Here's a quick once-over:

Ratio (or rate): a comparison of two amounts. If a family consists of two males and three females, the ratio of males to females is two to three.

Written as:	2 to 3, 2 : 3, or ⅔
Read as:	"Two to three."

Proportion: an equation showing that two ratios are equal.

Written as:	⅔ = 6/9
Read as:	"Two is to three as six is to nine."

Percent: a ratio showing how many per (out of) one hundred (25% = .25 = $^{25}/_{100}$ or ¼).

Written as:	25%
Read as:	"Twenty-five percent."

Common Fractions as Percents:

¹⁄₁₀ = 10%
⅕ = 20%
¼ = 25%
½ = 50%
¾ = 75%

HAVE MORE TIME?

➤ "Who has the biggest head?" Pose this question at the dinner table. After a lively discussion about your family members' physiques and the meaning of "a big head," redirect the discussion by asking, "Who has the biggest head *in proportion to* the rest of his or her body?" Follow your family's suggestions for ways to figure out the answer; for example, with ratios comparing the circumference of each person's head to his or her height. The results might be surprising, especially if you have a baby in the family!

➤ Draw percent designs. Make copies of page 206 or outline a ten-by-ten box on graph paper. Make sure your child realizes there are one hundred squares on the page or in the box. Ask your child to color in any number of squares in any design he wants. Then ask, "What percent of the squares have you colored in?" Next, suggest that your child make a mosaic design using as many different colors as he wants. After admiring the design, ask, "What percent of the squares did you color red [or blue or purple . . .]?"

➤ Play with analogies (analogies are actually word forms of ratios).
  • Winter *is to* cold *as* summer *is to* hot.
  • 3 *is to* 4 *as* 6 *is to* 8.
  • Make up analogies for your child to solve, and encourage your child to make up his own.

➤ Cook by ratios. Many recipes call for ratios: "3 cups of water per 1 cup of rice" or "2 ounces of spaghetti per person." Suggest that your child mix together ingredients such as cereal, raisins, nuts, or chocolate chips to create a recipe for a special snack. Have him record his recipe in ratios. Is it three parts chocolate chips to one part nuts, or one part chocolate chips to three parts nuts?

➤ Take your pulse. Have your child take his pulse for fifteen seconds. What is the ratio of his heartbeat per minute? Next, have him run in place or do jumping jacks for a couple of minutes and take his pulse again. How has the ratio of his heartbeat per minute changed?

➤ Calculate sales tax. Explain to your child how sales tax is computed in your state. What goods are taxed? What percentage of the price is added? Give your child an imaginary $100 to spend and have him look through catalogs or advertising circulars for items he would like to buy. Have him compute the total cost of the items with tax. How much money did he end up "spending" in tax?

Probability and Statistics

Walk along a hallway in any elementary school and you are bound to see at least one bulletin board full of graphs and charts. Children in schools these days are collecting data, and lots of it. What's your favorite color? How many pets do you have? How many hours of television do you watch in a week?

Which Graph?

Organizing data into graphs makes it easier to "see" a problem, make a comparison, or predict an outcome. Different kinds of graphs are more useful in some problem-solving situations than others.

- **Bar Graphs** enable people to compare a number of different quantities.
- **Circle Graphs** show the relationship of parts to a whole.
- **Line Graphs** show the rate at which something happens.
- **Pictographs** use symbols to compare different quantities.

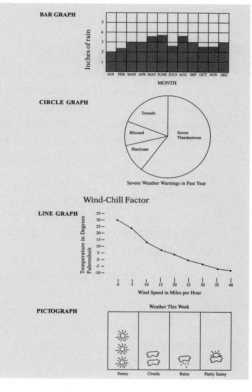

Children love collecting information, and by fifth grade they have the skills to organize it in a way that makes it possible to see relationships and draw conclusions from their statistical evidence. Fifth graders, in particular, seem to sense that their ability to understand the world around them rests on *information*. It is no wonder that you might find your fifth grader under the covers at night reading an almanac by flashlight. To a fifth grader, information is power.

Collecting information and estimating chances might seem more like play than like work. Still, do not underestimate their importance. Working with statistics provides a valuable context for applying computation skills. In this technological age, society increasingly relies on statistics and probability to make sense of the barrage of information available. Your child will need to know how to interpret statistics and predict outcomes in order to be able to make reasonable decisions in every aspect of her life.

This year, your child will continue to construct and interpret various types of graphs. She will learn to find the mean, median, and mode of a set of data, and will continue informal work in assigning probabilities. The more you talk about statistics and their uses at home, the more comfortable your child will be with these concepts at school and in the world beyond.

HAVE FIVE MINUTES?

➤ What *can't* you tell from a graph? Point out graphs in the daily newspaper or in magazines. Talk about the facts or comparisons the graphs are meant to show. Then ask, "What *doesn't* this graph tell you?" Discuss how different variables might affect the information given. For example, a graph might compare how fifth graders in different school districts scored on a standardized test, but it might *not* tell the time of year the test was given in each district.

➤ Guess the labels. Cut a graph out of a newspaper or magazine and cross out its labels. Ask your child, "What might this graph be about?" Challenge your child to come up with two different situations that the graph could describe.

➤ Investigate the state lottery. Buy a ticket and read the fine print. What are the odds of winning? How are the odds calculated? Why do the odds change from week to week? How much better is your chance of winning if you buy more tickets? Were there better ways you could have invested that dollar?

➤ Talk about combinations. The next time you are sorting laundry or packing for a trip, ask, "How many different outfits could you make with these two pairs of jeans and these three shirts?" Notice how your child goes about solving the problem and recording her findings.

➤ Compare products. At the grocery store or in the kitchen, point out the product information given on the labels of two different foods. Ask, "What are some different ways you could use these statistics to compare these products?" Talk about the statistics used to describe nutritional value, cost, shelf life, and other information about products.

➤ Roll the dice. Keep a pair of dice in your glove compartment or purse. In the dentist's waiting room or any other time you have a few minutes to kill, take out the dice and ask a question such as "What are my chances of rolling a number greater than three?" or "What are my chances of rolling doubles?" Have your child toss the dice and record each toss to see how close her estimation of the odds is to the actual results.

➤ Put expectations in perspective. Will your fifth grader get a spot in the starting lineup? What are the chances that she and her best friend will be in the same cabin at camp? Okay, so she hates where she sits at the dinner table—how many alternatives are there? Figuring out the probability that something will happen helps keep the situation in perspective. Encourage your child to set up an experiment, use a model, or make a diagram to help her figure out the odds.

HAVE MORE TIME?

➤ Analyze commercials. Remind your child that advertisers schedule commercials during shows that they think appeal to their target market. Ask her, "Think of the commercials that air during your favorite show. What kind of products do advertisers think you might want to buy?" Encourage your child to follow the procedure below to find out what kind of buyer advertisers think she is.
  1. Write down each product that is advertised during your favorite show. (If an ad is shown more than once, record both appearances.)
  2. Use the list to come up with general categories that describe the kinds of products advertised; for example, food, toys, other TV shows, and so on.
  3. Tally the number of ads that fall into each category.
  4. Make a bar graph showing the number of times ads in each category appeared during the show.

➤ Use probability to get the chores done. Whose turn is it to do the dishes tonight? Mark five slips of paper with five different colors and place them in a bag. Announce that the first person to pull out a red slip will do the dishes. Ask your child, "What's the probability that you will have to do the dishes tonight?" [1 in 5]. "Suppose Gramps pulls out a yellow slip and keeps it. Now what's your probability?" [1 in 4]. "What's the fairest way to do this experiment?" [replace the slips after each person picks one]. Encourage your child to set up different probability experiments for different chores.

➤ Keep track of personal statistics. How many hits has your child had in the last five Little League games? How many books has she read in the last six weeks? How many hours of homework has she had to complete each night? Help her graph the results and look for patterns. Has she been in a batting or reading slump? Why? What day of the week does she usually get the most homework? How might that information help her plan her time?

➤ Design a spinner. Help your child make a spinner as shown. Have her color different parts of the circle different colors. Ask your child to describe the chances of landing on each color; for example, "The chances of the spinner landing on green are one in three," or "The spinner is four times as likely to land on blue as on orange." How does the size of each part affect the likelihood that the spinner will land on that color?

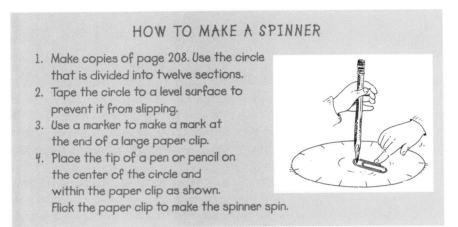

HOW TO MAKE A SPINNER

1. Make copies of page 208. Use the circle that is divided into twelve sections.
2. Tape the circle to a level surface to prevent it from slipping.
3. Use a marker to make a mark at the end of a large paper clip.
4. Place the tip of a pen or pencil on the center of the circle and within the paper clip as shown. Flick the paper clip to make the spinner spin.

➤ Calculate your family's food budget. Ask your child to estimate how much the family spends on food each week. Help her collect and tally the receipts for food purchases for a number of weeks. Does it make more sense to find the mean or the median amount spent each week? Why? How do your child's findings compare with her estimate?

➤ How would you describe your junk mail—statistically, that is? As you sort through your mail, hand pieces of junk mail to your child to tally. Have her record the day's total on a self-stick tag and place the tag where it won't get lost. At the end of a week, have her arrange the tags in order from least to greatest. Show your child how to remove tags in pairs, one from each end, to find the median amount of daily junk mail. Then replace the tags and ask her to give you the following statistics (see box on opposite page):

- the mean
- the maximum

- the minimum
- the mode

➤ Keep track of time. How does your child spend her day? For one 24-hour period, ask your child to keep track of how many hours she spends doing various activities such as sleeping, eating, going to school, taking lessons, or traveling from one place to another. Make a copy of page 208 and ask your child to use one of the circles to make a graph of her findings (note that one of the circles is divided into tenths and the other into twelfths). If she needs help, suggest that she round off her figures to the nearest hour.

Functions and Pre-algebra

Algebra? In fifth grade? Isn't algebra something you do in ninth grade? Why are the schools trying to rush your child?

Mean, Median, or Mode?

For many beginning (and not-so-beginning) statisticians, the most confusing part of working with statistics is understanding the vocabulary. Suppose a group of ten students got the following test scores. Here are a few of the terms that mathematicians might use to describe the data.

- **Maximum**—the largest number in a collection of data (100)
- **Minimum**—the smallest number in a collection of data (50)

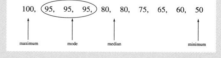

- **Range**—the difference between the maximum and the minimum (50)
- **Mode**—the number that appears most often (95)
- **Median**—the number in the middle when all numbers in the collection are ordered from greatest to least or least to greatest; if there are two middle numbers, the median is the average of those two numbers (80)
- **Mean**—the average of all the numbers; to find the mean, add all the numbers and then divide the sum by how many numbers were added $(100 + 95 + 95 + 95 + 80 + 80 + 75 + 65 + 60 + 50) \div 10 = 79.5$

Actually, your child has been working with the fundamentals of functions and algebra for a long time now. Every time your child recognized a pattern (red block, blue block, red block, blue block . . .), discovered a property of numbers ("Hey, if I know five times seven, then I know seven times five!"), or played a game of Battleship, he was setting the stage for the study of algebra and functions. Your child already knows that numbers and operation symbols are a useful shorthand for recording information. It is not uncommon for children in first and second grade to be asked to solve equations such as 3 + 2 = ? or for children in third grade to create What's My Rule? machines like this one:

	×3
1	3
2	6
3	9
4	

What happens in the upper grades—sometimes in fifth but almost certainly in sixth—is that this informal work is given a new set of names. Number sentences become *equations*. Patterns become *functions*. What you don't know becomes a *variable*. The numbers and their relationships remain the same. Your child is just modeling them in a different way.

Many fifth grade programs don't approach the study of equations and other algebraic concepts until the end of the year. Some don't approach it at all. By using the language of algebra as you and your child work with numbers, you can help your child be ready for these concepts when the time comes. (For additional activities that reinforce algebraic concepts, see Problem Solving, page 126, Number Sense and Whole Number Computation, page 138, and Geometry, page 154.)

HAVE FIVE MINUTES?

➤ Speak the language of algebra. Rather than saying "How old is your cousin Jill?" say "Let's say Jill is n years old. If you were born three years later, then your age would be n minus three. How old would that make her?"

➤ Play with patterns. Give your child six random numbers under 20. Can he create a pattern with them? Can you continue the pattern?

➤ Talk about formulas. Most fifth graders are familiar with at least one or two formulas; for example, $l \times w = A$ (length x width = area). Encourage your child to come up with formulas for everyday occurrences such as $p + s = t$ (puppy + Mom's slipper = trouble).

A New Language

As anyone who has tried to learn a foreign language will attest, the more you use a new language, the easier it is to learn. Here is a list of "vocabulary words" to help you get started in the language of algebra.

- **Algebraic Expression**— an expression that combines numbers and variables.
- **Equation**—a number sentence that expresses an equality; in equations, the relationship between numbers is represented by = ("equals" or "is equal to"). $3 + 2 = 5$ is an equation.
- **Inequality**—a number sentence that expresses an unequal relationship; in inequalities, the relationship is represented by < ("is less than") or > ("is greater than"). $3 + 2 < 7$ is an inequality.
- **Variable**—a symbol (usually a letter) that stands for a number. In the equation $3 + n = 5$, n is a variable.
- **Open Sentence**—a number sentence that contains a variable. $3 + n = 5$ is an open sentence.
- **Solution**—any number that makes an open sentence true.

➤Toss out a problem. While you're waiting in line or at the bus stop, toss out a problem such as $2x + y = 10$. Talk about the meaning of the equation (2 times one number plus another number equals 10). Then see how many solutions for x and y you and your child can find before the bus comes.

➤Read *The Mysterious Multiplying Jar,* by Anno Mitsumasa (Philomel). Ask, "If I were to give you a penny and double your money every day, how long would it take for you to become a millionaire?" [27 days]

➤Play Silent Guess My Number. Have your child choose a number between 1 and 20. Try to guess the number by writing algebraic expressions that can be answered "Yes" or "No." In response, your child writes *yes* or an algebraic expression; for example:

> Parent: $n < 7$? (Is the number less than seven?)
> Child: Yes.
> Parent: $n = 5 + 1$?
> Child: $n > 5 - 1$

You may ask questions about equivalences; for example:
"Does it equal $7 + 3$?"
But if you ask the exact number ("Is it 10?") and you are incorrect, you lose.

HAVE MORE TIME?

➤ Puzzle your fifth grader with algebraic patterns. In both of the following patterns, n stands for the same number. Can you figure it out without doing the calculations?

$n \times 9 + 7 = 88$
$n \times 98 + 6 = 888$
$n \times 987 + 5 = 8,888$
$n \times 9,876 + 4 = 88,888$

$n \times 1 + 2 = 11$
$n \times 12 + 3 = 111$
$n \times 123 + 4 = 1,111$
$n \times 1,234 + 5 = 11,111$

➤ Grow crystals. On a sheet of graph paper or a copy of page 208, draw an x (horizontal) and a y (vertical) axis. Ask your child to color in squares to make a design that is symmetrical both horizontally and vertically. Ask, "What do you notice about the number of squares you have to color each time you make the crystal grow?"

➤ Create word equations. Ask your child to think of all the things that numbers can tell about him (his birthdate, his height, his weight, his shoe size, his address). Suggest that he use those numbers to make up word equations about himself; for example, "The year I was born plus my age equals this year."

➤ Play Make an Equation. Using any handy set of numbers, such as the numbers in an address or on a license plate, see who can be the first one to arrange the numbers in a true equation. You can use any operations and list the numbers in any order. The street number 2328, for example, might make the equation $2 \times 3 + 2 = 8$ or $8 - 2 = 2 \times 3$.

Solutions to brainteasers on page 136.

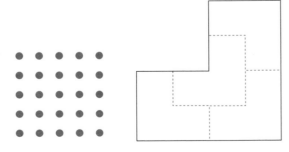
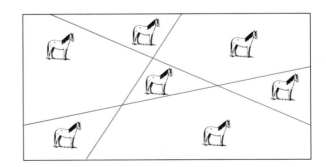

Working Below Grade Level in Math

If your child is struggling in math, the symptoms are probably all too familiar by now. Your child comes home complaining that she hates math, that she just doesn't get it, or that it is boring or too complicated. Homework becomes a war zone of tears and frustration. Math papers get "lost" or come home covered in red ink. Worse yet, your child decides that she just isn't good in math and just stops trying.

If you are worried about your child's performance in math, the time to take action is now. Fifth grade is a critical year in mathematics. In many school districts, it is the last year that students can catch up on lagging computation skills before moving into what is formally known as pre-algebra in the middle school years. If your child has missed fundamental concepts along the way, she has probably already started to "fake it" by learning isolated tricks that help her get through each day's lesson without really understanding what is going on. This method of getting by works well up to a point, but it can't hold up much longer. The nervousness and avoidance that result from a fundamental lack of understanding of how numbers work are the hallmarks of what is popularly known as math anxiety. If your child is anxious about math, she will choose to avoid math and math classes, which will in turn severely limit her choices not only in school but in life.

Okay, so you need to act, but what do you do? Here are a few suggestions.

- Listen to your child. It might be difficult to stop and listen during a battle over homework, but try to give your child the opportunity to be heard. If your child shouts "I just don't get this!" express sympathy ("Yeah, this is a tough one") and then try to get down to specifics ("What part is confusing you?").
- Gather information. Find out as much as you can about your child's math program. If possible, sit in on a class or two. If your child has a math text, take some time to look through it. Is the emphasis on learning computation methods or do the children tend to do more investigative problem solving? Does your child seem bored or confused by the methods being used?
- Troubleshoot. Become an active ally of your child's teacher. Ask *specific* questions about your child's progress. Are your child's difficulties with division common at the beginning of fifth grade, or is she lagging behind the others in the class? If your child is clearly lagging behind, what resources or services are available for remedial work? A learning disorder, such as attention deficit disorder or dyslexia, might be affecting your child's memory, organizational skills, or reading ability—each a very important aspect of your child's ability to learn mathematics. If you or your child's teacher suspects that there is a problem, find out who can help you diagnose the problem and make that appointment now.
- Do *not* attempt to "reteach" your child. Your child is probably trying her hardest to "do it the right way." If your method conflicts with the method your child is learning at school, it might only serve to add to her confusion and frustration.
- Continue to do everything you can to make math fun at home. Even if you have a very strong aversion to math yourself, do your best not to pass on a negative attitude (see Problem Solving, page 126). Involve your child in activities that connect mathematical learning to real problems in the real world. If necessary, give your child concrete objects to help her make the necessary connections. However, try to avoid the temptation to buy "skill-boosting" workbooks. For the child who is struggling to complete workbook pages at school, more of the same at home is the quickest way to kill his interest in or success with math.
- Consider hiring a tutor. As your child enters preadolescence, your own abilities to help her might be diminished by both her struggle for independence and your lack of familiarity with math concepts or teaching methods. Hiring a tutor does *not* mean relinquishing responsibility, however. You are still the most important influence in your child's life, and the time you spend just talking about mathematical ideas is more precious than gold. Don't give it up.

- Find like minds. Whatever your child's difficulty in math is—from simple boredom to a specific learning disability—a support group can be invaluable. Talk to other parents and to teachers. Ask around to find out who in your school is keen about math. If there doesn't seem to be anyone, call the middle school or the high school, or ask the school counselor to recommend someone who can give you a good lead.
- Look into groups outside of school that sponsor math programs. Girls' and Boys' Clubs, Scouts, community centers, and after-school groups all might have programs that will stimulate your child's interest in math.
- Family Math is a program that brings parents and children together to explore and enjoy math. If there is no program in your area, check out the book *Family Math,* by Jean Stenmark, Virginia Thompson, and Ruth Cossey (University of California), or the Family Math website at http://theory.lcs.mit.edu:80/~emjordan/famMath.html.

Math Enrichment

Does this scene sound familiar? You are patiently trying to explain how to invert and multiply fractions, and your child is telling you that his favorite stock is up 2¾. Or you are talking to him about multiplying decimals, and he is busy comparing money market funds. Or you are explaining what an isosceles triangle is, and he's using Pythagorean theory to figure out the height of the oak tree in the front yard. For some children, math seems to be the most reasonable way of dealing with the world. By fifth grade, if your child is ahead of the class in math, he might, indeed, be way ahead of you. How can you support his needs?

- First, make sure that your child is challenged and enjoying math in school. This might or might not mean placing him in a talented or gifted program, and it certainly does not mean separating him to allow him to "work at his own speed." Even if your child is more adept than some at coming up with the right answers, he still needs the important by-products of good teaching: learning to follow classroom routines, learning to work within a group, and learning to communicate ideas, to name a few.
- Second, give your child a chance to play. Remember that "more challenging" does not necessarily mean "more work." Make sure that your child has opportunities to be actively involved with other children solving the problems that naturally arise in the course of figuring out rules to a game or completing a craft project. Working things out with peers will teach

your child to respect the contributions of others and appreciate that there are many different ways to solve a problem.

- Third, look into math opportunities outside of school. Visit museums and libraries. Ask if your school sponsors an Odyssey of the Mind program. Check with your local high school or community college to find other resources that are available. Hunt down or organize your own Family Math program (see page 177).

- Finally, remember that your child's attitude toward math and his confidence in his abilities ultimately come from you. Just as a good reader still needs to be read to, a good math student still needs lots of opportunities to "do math" with the most important person in his life—you.

HAVE FIVE MINUTES?

➤ What's the date? The twenty-sixth? See how many interesting ways your child can come up with that number; for example, "What's the probability of picking a black two from a deck of cards? One in ___." For a wealth of daily ideas, check out the *Children's Mathematics Calendar*, by Theoni Pappas (Wide World Publishing).

➤ Create mazes. Have your child trace his hand or foot and create a maze out of it for you to solve. Or build a giant maze in sand or snow or playground gravel. But watch out: fifth grade mazes can be tough.

There are hundreds of maze books available in the library and bookstores, and many games magazines contain them as well. If your child is interested, here are a few good ones to start him off:

- *3-Dimensional Lateral Logic Mazes*, by Larry Evans (Sterling Publications)
- *Citymaze: A Collection of Amazing City Mazes*, by Wendy Madgwick (Millbrook)
- *Explor-A-Maze*, by Robert Snedden (Millbrook)
- *The Great Double Maze Book*, by Juliet Snape and Charles Snape (Harry M. Abrams)

➤ Create a dice game. Give your child a pair of dice—or better yet, a few pair—and ask him to come up with a new game of dice.

Curl Up with a Good Book

If you feel that your child needs a greater challenge than you can provide, don't rush out to buy the last overachiever workbook series. There is excellent children's literature available that presents mathematical topics in intriguing and enjoyable ways. Look for these and other books in your library or local bookstore and share them with your child. You might learn something.

- *Cool Math*, by Christi Maganzini (Price Stern Sloan)
- *How Do They Do That?* and others, by Caroline Sutton (William Morrow)
- *If You Made a Million*, and others, by David Schwartz (Lothrop, Lee and Shepard)
- *Math for Kids and Other People Too!* and others, by Theoni Pappas (Wide World Publishing)
- *Math for Smartypants* and others, by Marilyn Burns (Little, Brown)
- *The Mysterious Multiplying Jar* and others, by Anno Mitsumasa (Philomel)
- *The Phantom Tollbooth*, by Norton Juster (Bullseye)
- *The Toothpaste Millionaire*, by Jean Merrill (Houghton Mifflin)
- *When Do Fish Sleep?* and Other Imponderables, by David Feldman (HarperCollins)

➤ Read a mini-mystery together and test your powers of deductive reasoning. Check your library or bookstore for books of mini-mysteries, such as
- *Baffling Whodunit Puzzles: Dr. Quicksolve Mini-Mysteries,* by Jim Sukach (Sterling)
- *Baker Street Puzzles,* by Tom Bullimore (Sterling)
- *Five-Minute Mysteries,* by Ken Weber (Running Press)
- *Great Book of Whodunit Puzzles,* by Falcon Travis (Sterling)

➤ Recite an old rhyme. Chaos theory might be a newly coined phrase, but its meaning is as old as this old folk rhyme:

> For want of a nail, the shoe was lost;
> For want of a shoe, the horse was lost;
> For want of a horse, the rider was lost;
> For want of a rider, the battle was lost;
> For want of a battle, the kingdom was lost.

Discuss the meaning of the rhyme. Then encourage your child to come up with his own version; perhaps, "For want of a missing sneaker . . ."

HAVE MORE TIME?

➤ Investigate mathematical knots. Believe it or not, there is a whole branch of mathematics devoted to knots (try looking up "knots" on an Internet search machine). Mathematical knots are knots with no loose ends. You can connect the ends of a piece of rope with duct tape—or, better yet, use an extension cord and just plug one end into another. Here is a simple mathematical knot to get you started.

➤ Make geometric models. Have your child trace and cut out the pattern below. Encourage him to experiment with folding the pattern to form a cube. (You can connect the sides with tape to hold the cube in place.) Challenge your child to come up with patterns of his own to make solids such as
- a **tetrahedron** (four triangular faces)
- an **octahedron** (eight triangular faces)
- a **dodecahedron** (twenty regular pentagons as faces)

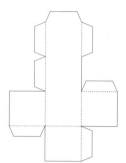

➤ Put on a magic show. Encourage your child to get together with a few friends and create a full-fledged magic show. By now, your fifth grader has most of the mathematical skills and the strength of memory to pull off fairly elaborate tricks with cards, coins, and other magicians' paraphernalia (no sawing people in half, however). Look in your library or bookstore for books of magic tricks. After the kids have polished their show, encourage them to hire themselves out as entertainment for younger children's birthday parties.

➤ Make and use an abacus. The abacus is a calculating tool invented by the Chinese thousands of years ago. Encourage your child to use the library to find out as much as possible about how an abacus works. Better still, if you happen to live near a Chinese community, visit a shop or other commercial enterprise where abacuses are still in use. Suggest that your child make an abacus of his own. He can find excellent directions in the book *Math Wizardry for Kids,* by Margaret Kenda and Phyllis S. Williams (Barrons), or he can use craft sticks, florist wire, and beads to make a simpler version. (*Math Wizardry* and the *World Book Encyclopedia* can both help if he gets stuck). Let your child know that there are many people throughout the world who feel that using the abacus is a faster means of performing calculations than using the calculator. What does he think?

➤ Perform science experiments. Math and science are inextricably linked. Each time your child performs even the simplest of experiments, he uses skills in measurement, data collection, and computation. There are many fine books of science experiments available for middle graders, such as *Explorabook: A Kid's Science Museum in a Book,* by John Cassidy (Klutz Press). On the following page is an example of a quick and easy exploration your child can do at home.

DISTILLING WATER

Present the following problem to your child: "Suppose you were shipwrecked in the middle of the ocean and had no fresh water to drink. How could you make fresh water out of the salt water that is all around you?" Then have him follow these steps.

1. Pour half a cup of salt water into a large bowl. Place a smaller bowl inside the large bowl. If necessary, place a rock inside the small bowl to weigh it down.
2. Cover the large bowl with a sheet of plastic wrap and tape the edges to make sure it is airtight.
3. Place a small marble or pebble in the middle of the plastic wrap so that it is slightly indented.
4. Leave the bowls in a sunny spot for a couple of days.
5. After a few days, compare the taste of the water in the small bowl to the taste of the water in the large bowl.

Working with Your Child's Teacher

....

This book and the accompanying assessment can provide you with lots of information about fifth grade expectations and how your own child is progressing toward meeting those expectations. There is, however, much information about your child's schooling that this book cannot provide.

This book cannot tell you, for example, the methods your child's teacher uses to teach fifth grade skills. Does she teach to the whole group, to small groups, or to individuals? Does she encourage children to work together or does she ask them to work alone—or does she do both? The book also cannot tell you the sequence in which the skills will be taught or integrated into the curriculum. Will decimals be introduced in the beginning of the year or at the end? What math skills will be incorporated into the thematic unit on Japan?

No book can tell you exactly how your child's performance is being measured and recorded this year since assessment methods vary greatly from school to school and from classroom to classroom. Nor can any book give you a clear picture of how your child interacts in the classroom (you might discover that your child can behave quite differently in a different setting) or how your child is doing socially. Both of these factors greatly affect school success.

To gather this kind of information you must form a strong line of communication with your child's teacher. Most schools provide several ways for teachers and parents to share information, but you might discover that you will glean far more information if you take the lead now and then. Here are some ways in which you can get a closer look at your child's learning experience.

Open House

Open House, also known as Parents' Night or Back-to-School Night, is an evening set aside for teachers to present their goals, methods of instruction, and routines. The purpose of this event is not to discuss individual students but to introduce the program and classroom procedures as a whole.

Open House presentations are as varied as the personalities of the teachers who give them. Your child's teacher might present you with a brief written description of his expectations, or he might simply invite you to come into the room and look around. He might have you participate in some of the math and reading activities the children do, or he might even have prepared a video or a slide show to demonstrate a typical day in fifth grade.

If your child's teacher has not prepared an elaborate or particularly detailed presentation, remember that not all teachers are extroverts. Many feel far more comfortable in a room with twenty-five rambunctious ten-year-olds than in front of a group of adults. If this is true of your child's teacher, try posing a few encouraging questions to help the teacher provide you and other appreciative parents with more detailed information.

"But," you might say, "what if I am not an extrovert either? And besides, I don't want the teacher to think I'm an overbearing or uncooperative parent!" Indeed, many parents find that they are more anxious on Parents' Night than the teachers are. The parents' own experiences as students or their lingering fear of authority can cause trepidation. After all, whose heart doesn't beat a little faster at the thought of being sent to the principal's office? Simply meeting the person with whom your child will spend over 180 days this year can be unnerving enough to cause you to sit passively at your child's desk.

Keep in mind that *how* you pose your questions can make a difference. Questions need not be challenges. They can be invitations. "What does the study of constellations have to do with spelling?" is a challenge. "Your study of constellations sounds fascinating. Can you tell us more about how you will integrate spelling skills into that study?" on the other hand, is an invitation to discussion. Most teachers are passionate about children and the subjects they teach. Encourage your child's teacher to expound on what excites him most.

Parent Conferences

There are three kinds of parent-teacher conferences: regularly scheduled conferences, special conferences that you initiate, and special conferences that your child's teacher initiates. The purpose of each of these conferences is the same: to discuss how your child is doing and how you can support him emotionally and educationally. Your role in each of these conferences, however, might vary depending on who initiated the conference.

Scheduled Conferences

Scheduled conferences usually occur once at the beginning of the school year and once later on in the year. Before attending a scheduled conference, you'll want to do some data gathering. Remember, the more information you have going into a conference, the easier the conference will be for everyone. Begin with your child. Long before conference time, you should be asking specific questions. "How's school going?" might not elicit much of a response. However, specific questions, such as those below, might prompt a more meaningful response:

- "What are you working on in math?"
- "What's your favorite thing to do in class? Why?"
- "What do you like best [or least] about language arts?"
- "Does your teacher give you specific feedback about your writing?"
- "What worries you about school?"

Next, think about learning activities you and your child have done together and any questions the activities have raised. If you have given your child the assessment in this book, you might find that you already have a number of questions. For instance, you might have observed that your child approaches math problems by recalling a procedure: "First I do this. Then I do this." Even if the teacher reports that your child is doing well in math, you might want to discuss whether your child is memorizing ways to solve problems or whether he truly understands the way fractions or decimals work. Tell the teacher what you have observed at home and see if your observations match the teacher's.

As you prepare the questions you wish to ask your child's teacher, be aware that the teacher herself is preparing to meet with more than twenty sets of parents. It is likely that she has established a routine, such as showing you samples of your child's work or the results of formal and informal assessments. She might have one or two issues she wishes to bring to your attention. Because of the uniformity of these conferences, you might find yourself wondering if the teacher truly knows your child. A comment such as "Your son is such a pleasure to have in class" is nice to hear. But it is not nearly as useful—and ultimately as cherished—as "Your son has begun to use puns and figurative language in his writing. He demonstrates a sophisticated use of words." To elicit more specific comments about your child, feel free to ask questions like these:

- "In what areas have you seen the most growth? The least?"
- "How does my child's performance compare with that of other children at this grade level?" Teachers understandably do not like to compare children and are often reluctant to answer this question, but it is an important one. Keep in mind that you need to know about your child's progress and performance. The teacher might tell you that your child is growing daily as a reader. However, until you know that the growth that is taking place is in the lowest reading group, you have only half of the picture.
- "What are my child's work habits like?"
- "What are my child's interests?"
- "What motivates my child in school?"
- "Does my child have close and consistent friends? What are they like?"
- "How would you describe my child's attention span?"
- "What can I be doing at home to help support my child's learning?"

If during the conference the teacher uses jargon you're not familiar with or if the teacher describes your child in ways that seem vague, ask for clarification. "A live wire" could mean that your child is bright and curious or that he has difficulty sitting still or paying attention. Try not to leave the conference until you are sure you have a clear picture.

Most routine conferences are scheduled in fifteen- to twenty-minute blocks (which is why you want to be on time for yours). If your conference is coming to an end and you have just unearthed an area of concern, ask to schedule another conference. Most teachers will be happy to do so.

You might find that your child is invited or expected to attend your teacher's conference with you. This format has both advantages and disadvantages. By attending the conference, your child will be encouraged to take a more active role in his own learning and assessment. You might, however, have questions you would like to discuss with the teacher privately. If your child has been asked to attend, and you do not want to discuss all of your concerns in his presence, request a second conference time or indicate that you will be following up with a phone call.

When You Initiate a Conference

Although you might be tempted to seek information from the teacher during a class field trip or while you're dropping your child off at school after a dentist's appointment, try to refrain from doing so. Impromptu discussions about one child's progress are too much to ask of a teacher who's fully immersed in teaching. Instead, if you have concerns or wish to know more about your child's learning, make an appointment to see the teacher or speak with her on the telephone.

You might want to schedule a conference or phone call to inform the teacher of any stresses or special circumstances your child is experiencing. Illness, parental separation or divorce, death of a dear one (including pets), and particular fears can all affect a child's school experience and are well worth revealing to the teacher. It is also appropriate to schedule a conference if you have noticed confusing or unwarranted changes in your child's behavior. You and the teacher might be able to pull together enough information to make sense of the change.

By fifth grade social concerns have moved to the forefront. It's easy for a fifth grader to become overly preoccupied with the making and keeping of friendships. A certain amount of turmoil—good days and bad—is normal in the social arena. But if your child is having difficulty with peers, if he is seemingly without friends and longs for them, or if he's being harassed or ostracized on a regular basis, do not hesitate to schedule a time to talk to his teacher. Some schools see an increase in casual violence—pushing, shoving, verbal abuse—at this stage. This should never be brushed off by the teacher or the principal in a "kids will be kids" fashion. Social acceptance is not an individual problem—it is a community problem. Together, you and your child's teacher can brainstorm appropriate strategies to teach your child and others methods for optimum success in dealing with conflict.

At times, your concerns might have less to do with your child's individual progress than with the classroom situation as a whole. Perhaps you take issue with a specific method your child's teacher is using, or you would like to see learning addressed in other ways. Parents often hesitate to talk to teachers about these considerations for fear that the teacher will feel attacked and subsequently take her anger out on their children. This common fear is rarely warranted. Teachers know that listening and responding to parents will ultimately bring about more support, not less. In most situations a parent's concern, particularly a first-time concern, is taken quite seriously, especially if your choice of words and tone of voice are cooperative rather than confrontational. In schools, as in other institutions, the squeaky wheel does get the grease. Scheduling a conference and expressing your concern in a genuine spirit of collaboration are appropriate.

If you have a concern about your child and are wondering if you should set up a conference, do so, and do it *now* (October is not too soon). It is far better to communicate early, when both you and your child's teacher can be proactive rather than reactive. Address the problem *before* your child experiences frustration or a sense of failure. Success is the leading motivator in school achievement. Don't let your child lose that feeling of success.

When the Teacher Initiates a Conference

Suppose you come home from work to find a message on your answering machine: Your child's teacher wants to have a conference. Like any parent, you assume the worst. First comes the flood of questions for your child: "How are things going at school? Any problems?" Next comes the steady flow of parental guilt: What have I failed to do?

Don't panic. Find out the specific purpose of the meeting. Who knows? Your child's teacher might simply want to talk to you about a volunteer position in the classroom or about your child's special talents. If she seems reluctant to give you details before the meeting, understand that this is to prevent an immediate and full-range discussion at the time of the phone call. In truth, it is probably more advantageous for everyone involved to wait, process the information, and be prepared at the meeting. To find out the purpose of the meeting, you might say, "I know that we don't have time to discuss the issue now, but could you tell me in a few words what the conference will be about?" Then ask who, other than the teacher, will attend the conference. Finally, ask, "Is there a helpful way that I can prepare?" This last question will set the right tone, indicating that you are open and eager to work together.

If two parents are involved in your child's education, try to arrange for both to attend the conference. This way one parent will not end up trying to communicate information secondhand, and everyone can become involved in a plan of action. Be sure to arrange a means for following up as well. You might want to set up a regular system of communication—sending notes back and forth, perhaps, or calling every Friday. Some teachers even suggest keeping a "dialogue journal" in which the parent and teacher exchange progress reports and observations in a notebook that the child carries to and from school.

Whether you initiate a conference or the teacher does, remember that the main purpose of any conference is to collect and share essential information. More often than not, teachers are relieved when parents bring problems to their attention. You, too, should be glad that a problem has been noticed and addressed. At the very least, by opening a vital line of communication, you and the teacher will clarify important views pertaining to the education of your child.

Student Assessment

When you went to school there were probably two types of assessments: tests and report cards. The same holds true for many schools today. In some schools, primary students do not take tests, except perhaps for the weekly spelling test, but they do get report cards. The report card might have letter grades, it might be a checklist, or it might be an anecdotal report. In still other schools new methods of evaluation called "performance-based testing" or "authentic assessment" use anecdotal records, learning journals, and portfolios as a means of reporting progress. A third type of assessment is the standardized test. Each of these types of assessment looks at learning from one or more angles, and all can be helpful to you and your child—if you understand the benefits and limitations of each form.

Report Cards

Report cards are often considered a conclusion: How well did your child do this quarter? How hard did she try? Many types of report cards, however, raise more questions than they answer. If your child gets grades, you might find yourself wondering what a B really means. Is your child performing slightly above average for the whole class? Or is your child performing slightly above average in her math group? Can a child in the lowest math group get a B? If your child doesn't get traditional letter grades, but receives an O for Outstanding, S for Satisfactory, and N for Needs improvement, you might still be left wondering what constitutes an outstanding grade as opposed to a satisfactory grade.

Some schools are moving toward more informative report cards. These usually include a checklist of skills and learning behaviors and are marked according to how often your child exhibits those behaviors (Consistently, Most of the Time, Sometimes, Not Yet). The checklist might also be accompanied by anecdotal records. Remember, the perfect reporting device for all children has yet to be devised. Report cards are designed for parents, so if the reports in your district do not meet your needs, let the principal know.

No matter what type of report card your child receives, try to use it as a springboard rather than as a conclusion. As a springboard, a report card gives you the opportunity to talk with your child. Here are some suggestions:

- Ask your child what she thinks of her progress report. Listen to her feelings and guide her in assessing how well she thinks she's doing.
- First and foremost, praise your child for things done well. In fact, you might want to concentrate only on the positive in your first reaction to a report card.
- If you and your child can see a place that needs improvement, talk about *how* your child could go about improving. Telling him to try harder or giving him incentives (a dollar for every A) is probably not helpful. He cannot improve without a clear understanding of what is expected of him and how he can work on the problem. If you have already pinpointed a need using the assessment in this book, the report card can provide an

opportunity to reinforce the good work you have already begun to do together.

- If you have questions about the report card or if you need further clarification, schedule a conference with your child's teacher.

Above all, keep your discussion with your child as upbeat and positive as possible. Remember, report cards can tear down what your child needs most: confidence. So, as your child's main coach, review the report card but don't let it define her or give her the impression that your love or respect is based on her ability. Your child is not an A or a C student. She is what we all are, a continuous learner.

Performance-Based Assessment

In many schools, teachers are pushing for changes in assessment. They realize that learning does not occur just at the end of a unit or at the end of a marking period. It is happening all the time. In these schools teachers are keeping records while observing children at work. They talk to children about what they know and how they approach problems. In addition, both students and their teachers often save the work that demonstrates learning and keep it in a portfolio.

A portfolio is a collection of work. It might contain several writing samples (usually the rough drafts in addition to the finished product to show growth), charts and descriptions that show how a child approached a math or science project, drawings or other artwork, and a report or project done over time. Sometimes the teacher chooses what will go into the portfolio, sometimes the child decides, and sometimes they select the work together. In any case, the student is usually asked to do some self-assessment.

Most parents find that a portfolio is a good source of information about their child's progress and school expectations. They are able to see the quality of their child's thinking, the effort that was applied, and the outcomes. While reviewing a portfolio, parents and teachers can discuss future goals for the child.

If your child's teacher isn't using a portfolio method, but regularly sends home completed work, you can assemble your own portfolio. Some parents buy artists' portfolios for this purpose; others use accordion files or date the work and keep it in a cardboard box. Study the work in the portfolio for signs of how your child is progressing. Go beyond the teacher's comments at the top of the paper and look instead for changes in your child's work. Praise her for applying new concepts and showing what she knows. As you do the exercises in this book, keep work that demonstrates growth. These may come in handy when you are discussing your child's needs with the teacher.

Standardized Testing

Chances are, your fifth grader has already had experience with standardized testing. Standardized tests are considered "objective" because they are administered in the same manner, with the same directions, to children at the same grade level all across the country. They measure student performance in norms, percentiles, and stanines that allow children to be compared to other children, and schools to be compared with other schools. The results of standardized tests can be used, and are used, in a number of different ways. Some of the most common uses are: to determine the strengths and weaknesses of a school's educational program; to inform teachers and parents about the academic growth of individual students; and to identify children who might have learning problems or who might need a more challenging school experience (standardized test scores are often used to select children who need additional support at either end of the learning continuum).

If your child will participate in standardized testing this year, prepare her by briefly discussing the purpose of the test in a low-key manner—"the test will help your teacher decide what to teach next and help your teacher teach you well." It's in your child's best interest not to put too much emotional weight on the test or the test results. If you are anxious, you will likely convey that anxiety to your child, and any undue tension can hinder test performance.

Most schools that use standardized testing send the results to the students' parents. When you receive your child's scores, read the directions carefully to learn how to interpret them. If you have questions about the different numbers, ask the school principal to explain them. Don't be embarrassed or intimidated. Teachers often get a crash course in deciphering the code each year.

If your school doesn't send the results home, and you would like to know how your child fared, call the principal. If the test booklet becomes part of your child's school records, you are permitted by law to view it.

You might feel that the results accurately reflect what you know about your child. However, if you feel that there is a discrepancy between how your child performs in the classroom and how she performed on the test, speak to your child's teacher. Ask whether the results of the test are consistent with your child's performance. Keep in mind that many circumstances can affect test results. If your child didn't feel well, was unable to concentrate, or incorrectly interpreted the directions, the results will not be valid. If the teacher agrees that the test results are grossly inconsistent, and if the test results affect your child's education (determining reading or math group, for instance), you may request that your child take the test again. Testing companies can and will provide alternative tests.

Standardized tests can be useful to schools, teachers, and parents, but they can also be misused. Sometimes this limited—and, yes, flawed—form of measurement is used to determine whether a child should be promoted or retained, whether a child qualifies for special services, whether a teacher is successful, and whether a school system deserves to receive funds. But a standardized test should never be the sole basis of an important educational decision—particularly one that will affect individual children. Observational data and assessment of the child's teacher, parents, and sometimes specialists, should also be considered.

Observing Your Child in the Classroom

Undoubtedly the best way to collect information about your child's school experience is to observe the class in action. You might want to observe for a crucial hour, a morning, or a full day. With advance notice, most schools welcome parent observers. Send a note to your child's teacher (*not* the principal) first. Explain that you are working with your child at home and would like to learn more about the curriculum and her teaching methods. By watching, you'll be able to help your child in a way that is consistent with what the teacher is doing. Don't be shy about offering to help as well as observe—the more direct contact you have with the children, the better. Keep in mind that not every day is necessarily a good time to observe. The children might be at gym or participating in a special event. Also, most teachers would prefer you not come in September, when classroom routines and rules are just being established. Be aware, as well, that your child might not behave the same way while you are observing as he would if you were not present.

If possible, volunteer to help out in your child's classroom on a regular basis. Being a regular visitor will allow you, your child's teacher, and your child to relax into more normal behavior. Middle school is often the time when parents get the message that they are no longer needed or welcome in the classroom. This closed-door policy is neither good for schools nor good for your child. Consistently offer your services and work to build the teacher's trust in your presence.

While in the classroom, take your cues from the teacher and try not to offer suggestions too often. Let the teacher know how much you enjoy being in the classroom. If a concern arises, schedule a conference to talk with the teacher just as you would if you were not working side by side.

Even if you can't go in to school once a week, offer to go along on a field trip or to help out with a special project. As you work with your child's classmates, you will discover a great deal about how children learn at this grade level and you'll learn more about the school's academic goals. Your child will see firsthand how much you value education. His pride in your participation will go a long way toward helping him succeed in school.

Index

Activity Pages

The 5 W's

Who

Why

Where

What

When

Concentric Circles

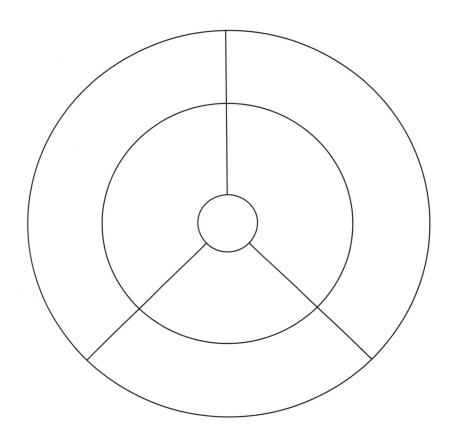

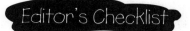
Editor's Checklist

Editor's Checklist

Skills	Date	Date	Date

Story Map

Title: _____

Author: _____

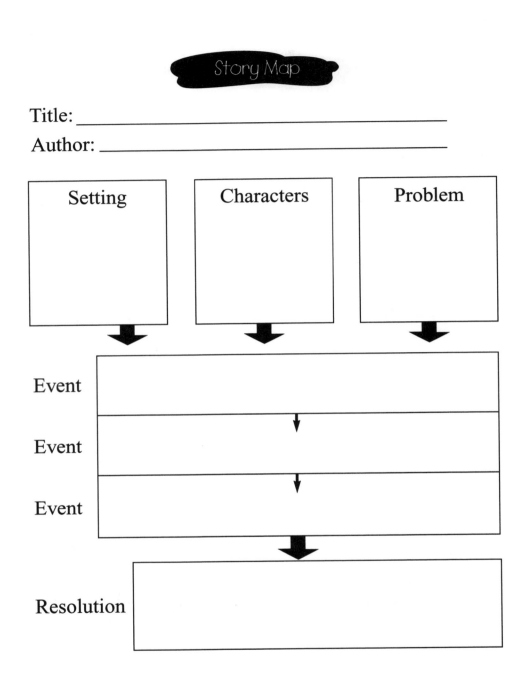

Setting

Characters

Problem

Event

Event

Event

Resolution

Fraction Strips

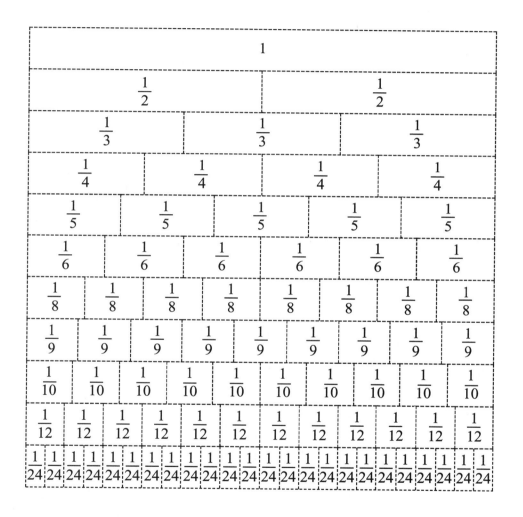

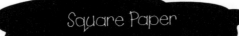

Square Paper

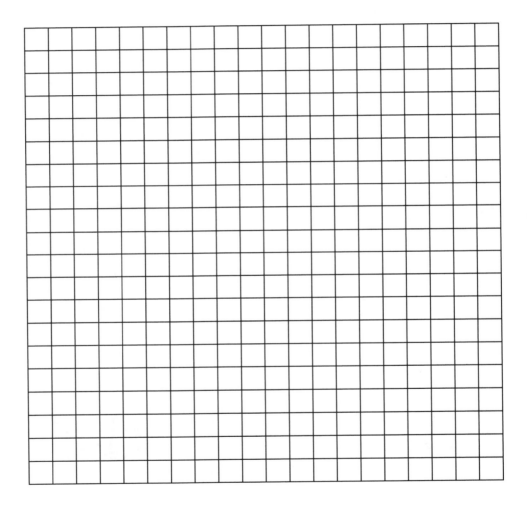

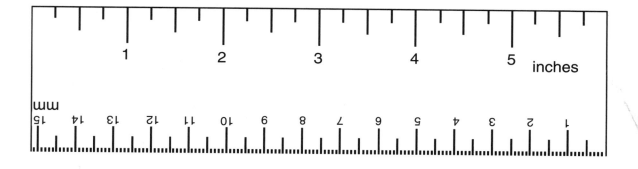

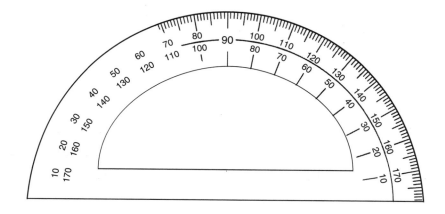

Circle Graphs

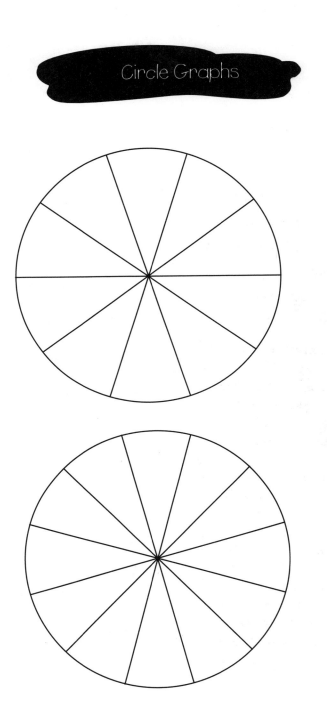